Department of Health and Welsh Office

CODE OF PRACTICE

Mental Health Act 1983

Published August 1993 pursuant to Section 118 of the Act

London: HMSO

FOREWORD

The law provides an essential framework for the care of those with a mental disorder – probably more than in any other area of health and social care. All professionals and managers working in this field need a sound working knowledge of mental health legislation and an understanding of the careful balance it represents between the individual rights of patients and society's responsibility to protect them and other people from the harm which mental disorder can cause. That is why this Code of Practice, issued under section 118 of the Mental Health Act 1983, is such an important document.

The first edition of the Code proved itself as an invaluable handbook for practitioners. The Mental Health Act Commission was entrusted with monitoring its operation and this second edition builds on the experience with the first, and on the wide range of responses from those consulted about the revision. We believe that it will command widespread confidence.

The legal framework, important though it is, remains a framework. As a Government we have given a very high priority to developing services for people who are mentally ill or who have a learning disability and to ensuring that community based care is effective. The Care Programme Approach, introduced in April 1991, is a key part of that commitment and is backed up by increasing resources devoted to this area, expansion of qualified staff (especially community psychiatric nurses) and specific measures such as the Homeless Mentally Ill initiative. This is a momentum we are determined to sustain. But these services will not be fully effective unless they are backed up by sensible and sensitive understanding and application of the legal provisions.

There is one special point we want to underline about the guidance in this new edition. It has been widely reported that the criteria for admission to hospital under the Act have not been correctly under-stood by all professionals. In particular, there is said to have been a misconception that patients may only be admitted under the Act if there is a risk to their own or other people's safety. In fact the Act provides for admission in the interests of the patient's health, or of his or her safety, or for the protection of other people. This is clearly spelt out in the new paragraph 2.6 of the Code.

Decisions about the care and treatment of any patient can only be taken in the light of his or her individual needs and circumstances. But it is vital that they are not distorted by misconceptions about a key provision of the Act.

We warmly commend the new Code. It is an essential guide for all those involved in caring for people with a mental disorder. We look to them to make the fullest use of it.

VIRGINIA BOTTOMLEY
SECRETARY OF STATE FOR HEALTH

JOHN REDWOOD
SECRETARY OF STATE FOR WALES

Contents

TREATMENT AND CARE IN HOSPITAL

LEAVING HOSPITAL

PARTICULAR GROUPS OF PATIENTS

1 Introduction

1.1 This revised Code of Practice has been prepared in accordance with section 118 of the Mental Health Act 1983 (the Act) by the Secretary of State for Health and the Secretary of State for Wales, after consulting such bodies as appeared to them to be concerned, and laid before Parliament. The Code will come into force on 1 November 1993. The Act does not impose a legal duty to comply with the Code but failure to follow the Code could be referred to in evidence in legal proceedings.

1.2 The Code imposes no additional duties on statutory authorities. Rather it provides guidance to statutory authorities, Managers (who have defined responsibilities under the provisions of the Act) and professional staff working in health (including mental nursing homes) and social services on how they should proceed when undertaking duties under the Act.

1.3 The Code provides much detailed guidance, but this needs to be read in the light of the following broad principles, that people being assessed for possible admission under the Act or to whom the Act applies should:

– receive respect for and consideration of their individual qualities and diverse backgrounds – social, cultural, ethnic and religious;

– have their needs taken fully into account though it is recognised that, within available resources, it may not always be practicable to meet them;

– be delivered any necessary treatment or care in the least controlled and segregated facilities practicable;

– be treated or cared for in such a way that promotes to the greatest practicable degree, their self determination and personal responsibility consistent with their needs and wishes;

– be discharged from any order under the Act to which they are subject immediately it is no longer necessary.

1.4 This means, in particular, that individuals should be as fully involved as practicable, consistent with their needs and wishes, in the formulation and delivery of their care and treatment, and that, where linguistic and sensory difficulties impede such involvement reasonable steps should be taken to attempt to overcome them. It means that patients should have their legal rights drawn to their attention, consistent with their capacity to understand them. Finally, it means that, when treatment or care is provided in conditions of security, patients should be subject only to the level of security appropriate to their individual needs and only for so long as it is required.

1.5 The Code has been made as comprehensive as possible, but inevitably gaps will emerge and amendments and additions to the Code will need to be made as appropriate in the light of experience. The Secretaries of State are required to keep the Code under review.

1.6 Finally a note on presentation. An attempt has been made to draft the Code in such a way as to make it acceptable not only to those for whom the Act requires it to be written but also many patients, their families, friends and supporters. Throughout the Code, the Mental Health Act 1983 is referred to as the Act. Where there is reference to sections of other Acts, the relevant Act is clearly indicated. The glossary (page 121) either defines some of the words in the Code or refers to relevant sections of the Act where definitions can be found. Following the style of the Act, the Code uses the terms 'he' and 'his' to encompass both male and female.

2 Assessment

General

2.1 This chapter is about the assessment by Approved Social Workers (A S Ws) and doctors of the needs of a person with mental health problems, where it may lead to an application for admission to hospital under the Mental Health Act 1983 (the Act).

2.2 Doctors and A S Ws must recognize that both have specific roles to play in assessment and should arrive at their own independent decisions. Such recognition should be underpinned by good working relationships based on knowledge and responsibilities; assessment should be carried out jointly unless good reasons prevent it (although it may be advantageous for each professional to interview the patient alone). An agreement should be reached between the professionals involved in the assessment process as to how their responsibilities can best be discharged.

2.3 A decision *not* to apply for admission under the Act should be clearly thought through, and supported, where necessary, by an alternative framework of care and/or treatment.

2.4 Everyone involved in assessment should be aware of the need to provide mutual support, especially where there is a risk of the patient causing serious physical harm (including, where necessary, the need to call for police assistance and how to use that assistance to minimise the risk of violence).

Assessment for possible admission under the Mental Health Act

2.5 The objectives of assessment under the Mental Health Act

All those assessing for possible admission under the Act should ensure that:

a.   they take all relevant factors into account;

b.   they consider and where possible implement appropriate alternatives to compulsory admission;

c.   they comply with the legal requirements of the Act.

The factors to be taken into account at assessment

2.6 A patient may be compulsorily admitted under the Act where this is necessary:

– in the interests of his own health, <u>or</u>

– in the interests of his own safety, <u>or</u>

– for the protection of other people.

Only one of the above grounds needs to be satisfied (*in addition to those relating to the patient's mental disorder*). However, a patient may only be admitted for treatment under section 3 if the treatment cannot be provided unless he is detained under the section. In judging whether compulsory admission is appropriate, those concerned should consider not only the statutory criteria but also:

– the patient's wishes and view of his own needs;

– his social and family circumstances;

– the risk of making assumptions based on a person's sex, social and cultural background or ethnic origin;

– the possibility of misunderstandings which may be caused by other medical/health conditions including deafness;

– the nature of the illness/behaviour disorder;

– what may be known about the patient by his nearest relative, any other relatives or friends and professionals involved, assessing in particular how reliable this information is;

– other forms of care or treatment including, where relevant, consideration of whether the patient would be willing to accept medical treatment in hospital informally or as an out-patient;

– the needs of the patient's family or others with whom the patient lives;

– the need for others to be protected from the patient;

– the impact that compulsory admission would have on the patient's life after discharge from detention;

– the burden on those close to the patient of a decision not to admit under the Act;

– the appropriateness of guardianship. (See Chapter 13).

Ordinarily only then should the applicant (in consultation with other professionals) judge whether the criteria stipulated in any of the admission sections are satisfied, and take the decision accordingly. In certain circumstances the urgency of the situation may curtail detailed consideration of all these factors.

Informal admission

2.7 Where admission to hospital is considered necessary and the patient is willing to be admitted informally this should in general be arranged. Compulsory admission should, however, be considered where the patient's current medical state, together with reliable evidence of past experience, indicates a strong likelihood that he will change his mind about informal admission prior to his actual admission to hospital with a resulting risk to his health or safety or to the safety of others.

Protection of others

2.8 In considering 'the protection of other persons' (see sections 2(2)(b) and 3(2)(c)) it is essential to assess both the nature and likelihood of risk and the level of risk others are entitled to be protected from, taking into account:

- reliable evidence of risk to others;

- any relevant details of the patient's medical history and past behaviour;

- the degree of risk and its nature. Too high a risk of physical harm, or serious persistent psychological harm to others, are indicators of the need for compulsory admission;

- the willingness and ability to cope with the risk, by those with whom the patient lives;

- the possibility of misunderstandings resulting from assumptions based on a person's sex, social and cultural background or ethnic origin and from other medical/health conditions including deafness,

The health of the patient

2.9 A patient may be admitted under sections 2 and 3 solely in the interests of his own health even if there is no risk to his own or other people's safety. Those assessing the patient must consider:

- any evidence suggesting that the patient's mental health will deteriorate if he does not receive treatment;

- the reliability of such evidence which may include the known history of the individual's mental disorder;

- the views of the patient and of any relatives or close friends, especially those living with the patient, about the likely course of his illness and the possibility of its improving;

- the impact that any future deterioration or lack of improvement would have on relatives or close friends, especially those living with the patient, including an assessment of his ability and willingness to copy;

- whether there are other methods of coping with the expected deterioration or lack of improvement.

Individual professional responsibility – the Approved Social Worker

2.10 It is important to emphasise that where an A S W is assessing a person for possible admission under the Act he has overall responsibility for co-ordinating the process of assessment and, where he decides to make an application, for implementing that decision. The A S W must, at the start of his assessment of the patient, identify himself to the patient, members of the family or friends present with the patient, and the other professionals involved in the assessment, explain in clear terms his role and the purpose of his visit, and ensure that the other professionals have explained their roles. A S Ws should carry with them at all times documents identifying them as A S Ws.

2.11 The A S W must interview the patient in a 'suitable manner'.

a. Where the patient and A S W cannot understand each other's language sufficiently, wherever practicable recourse should be had to a trained interpreter who understands the terminology and conduct of a psychiatric interview (and if possible the patient's cultural background).

b. Where another A S W with an understanding of the patient's language is available, consideration should be given to requesting him to carry out the assessment or assist the A S W assigned to the assessment.

c. Where the patient has difficulty either in hearing or speaking, wherever practicable an A S W with appropriate communication skills should carry out the assessment or assist the A S W initially assigned to the case. Alternatively the A S W should seek the assistance of a trained interpreter. Social services departments should issue guidance to their A S Ws as to where such assistance can be obtained.

d. The A S W should bear in mind the potential disadvantages of a patient's relative being asked to interpret. Where possible, a trained interpreter should be used in preference to a relative, neighbour or friend.

e. Where the patient is still unwilling or unable to speak to the A S W (despite assistance from interpreters) the assessment will

have to be based on whatever information the A S W can obtain
from all reliable sources, making allowance for the risk of false
assumptions based on a person's sex or ethnic origin, or other
forms of prejudice.

f.   It is not desirable for a patient to be interviewed through a closed
door or window except where there is serious risk to other
people. Where there is no immediate risk of physical danger to
the patient or to others, powers in the Act to secure access
(section 135) should be used.

g.   Where the patient is subject to the effects of sedative medication,
or the short-term effects of drugs or alcohol, the A S W should
consult with the doctor/s and, unless it is not possible because of
the patient's disturbed behaviour and the urgency of the case,
either wait until, or arrange to return when, the effects have
abated before interviewing the patient. If it is not realistic to wait,
the assessment will have to be based on whatever information
the A S W can obtain from all reliable sources.

2.12 The patient should ordinarily be given the opportunity of
speaking to the A S W alone but if the A S W has reason to fear
physical harm he should insist that another professional sees the
patient with him. If the patient would like another person (for
example a friend) to be with him during the assessment and any
subsequent action that may be taken, then ordinarily the A S W
should assist in securing that person's attendance unless the urgency
of the case or some other proper reason makes it inappropriate to do
so.

2.13 The A S W must attempt to identify the patient's nearest relative (see section 26 of the Act and paras 67–68 of the Memorandum),
and ensure that his statutory obligations (section 11) to the nearest
relative are fulfilled. In addition, the A S W should where possible:

a.   ascertain the nearest relative's views about the patient's needs
and his (the relative's) own needs in relation to the patient;

b.   inform the nearest relative of the reasons for considering an
application for admission under the Mental Health Act and the
effects of making such an application.

It is a statutory requirement to take such steps as are practicable to inform the nearest relative about an application for admission under section 2 and of his power of discharge (section 11(3)). Consultation by the A S W with the nearest relative about possible application for admission under section 3 or reception into guardianship is a statutory requirement unless it is not reasonably practicable or would involve unreasonable delay (section 11(4)). Circumstances in which the nearest relative need not be informed or consulted include those where the A S W cannot obtain sufficient information to identify the nearest relative or his location or where to do so would require an excessive amount of investigation. Practicability refers to the availability of the nearest relative and not to the appropriateness of informing or consulting the person concerned.

2.14 If the nearest relative objects to an application being made, for admission for treatment or reception into guardianship, it cannot proceed at that time. The A S W may then need to consider applying to the county court for the nearest relative's 'displacement' (section 29), and local authorities must provide proper assistance, especially legal assistance, in such cases. It is desirable for clear practical guidance on the procedures to be available, and this should be discussed with the relevant county courts.

2.15 Where the A S W is the applicant for the admission of a patient to hospital, he must discuss, in so far as the urgency of the case allows, with other relevant relatives and friends their views of the patient's needs, and should take them into account.

2.16 The A S W should consult wherever possible with other professionals who have been involved with the patient's care, for example home care staff or community psychiatric nurses (C P Ns).

2.17 When the A S W has decided whether or not he will make an application for admission he should tell (with reasons):

– the patient;

– the patient's nearest relative (whenever possible);

– the doctor/s involved in the assessment.

When an application for admission is to be made the A S W should start planning how the patient is to be conveyed to hospital (see Chapter 11).

Individual professional responsibility – the doctor

2.18 The doctor should:

a. decide whether the patient is suffering from mental disorder within the meaning of the Act (section 1) and assess its seriousness and the need for further assessment and/or medical treatment in hospital;

b. consider the factors set out above at para 2.6, discussing his views with the applicant and the other doctor involved;

c. specifically address the legal criteria for admission under the Mental Health Act and if he is satisfied provide a recommendation setting out those aspects of the patient's symptoms and behaviour which satisfy the legal criteria for admission;

d. ensure that, where there is to be an application for admission, a hospital bed will be available.

Medical examination

2.19 A proper medical examination requires:

– direct personal examination of the patient's mental state, excluding any possible preconceptions based on the patient's sex, social and cultural background or ethnic origin;

– consideration of all available relevant medical information including that in the possession of others, professional or non-professional.

Where the patient and doctor cannot understand each other's language the doctor should, wherever practicable, have recourse to a trained interpreter, who understands the terminology and conduct of a psychiatric interview (and if possible the patient's cultural background).

2.20 If direct access to the patient is not immediately possible, and it is not desirable to postpone the examination in order to negotiate access, the relevant powers in the Act must be invoked (section 135) or consideration given to calling the police in order to see if they would exercise any relevant lawful power of entry.

2.21 It may not always be practicable for the patient to be examined by both doctors at the same time; but they should always discuss the patient with each other.

2.22 It is desirable for both doctors to discuss the patient with the applicant. It is essential for at least one of them to do so.

Joint medical recommendations

2.23 Joint medical recommendation forms (forms 3 and 10) should only be used where the patient has been jointly examined by two doctors. It is desirable that they are completed and signed by both doctors at the same time.

2.24 In all other circumstances separate recommendation forms should be used (forms 4 and 11).

The second medical recommendation

2.25 Other than in exceptional circumstances, the second medical recommendation should be provided by a doctor with previous acquaintance of the patient. This should be the case even when the 'approved' doctor (who is, for example, a hospital based consultant) already knows the patient. Where this is not possible (for example the patient is not registered with a G P) it is desirable for the second medical recommendation to be provided by an 'approved' doctor (see paras 2.37 and 2.38).

A decision not to apply for admission

2.26 Most compulsory admissions require prompt action to be taken but it should be remembered that the A S W has up to 14 days from the date of first seeing the patient to make an application for admission for assessment or treatment. Where a decision not to apply for a patient's compulsory admission is taken the professional concerned must decide how to implement those actions (if any) which his assessment indicates are necessary to meet the needs of the patient including, for example, the referral to other social workers or services within the social services department. It is particularly important that any C P N concerned with the patient's care be fully involved in the taking of such decisions. The professionals must ensure that they, the patient and (with the patient's consent except where section 13(4) applies) the patient's nearest relative and any other closely connected relatives have a clear understanding of any alternative arrangements. It is good practice for such arrangements to be recorded in writing and copies made available to all those who need them (subject to the patient's right to confidentiality).

2.27 The A S W must discuss with the patient's nearest relative the reasons for not making an application. The A S W should advise the nearest relative of his right to apply and suggest that he consult with the doctors if he wishes to consider this alternative. Where, moreover, the A S W is carrying out an assessment at the request of the nearest relative (section 13(4)) the reasons for not applying for the patient's admission must be given to the nearest relative in writing. Such a letter should contain sufficient details to enable the nearest relative to understand the decision whilst at the same time preserving the patient's right to confidentiality.

Particular practice issues

Disagreements

2.28 Sometimes there will be differences of opinion between assessing professionals. There is nothing wrong with disagreements: handled properly these offer an opportunity to safeguard the interests of the patient by widening the discussion on the best way of meeting the patient's needs. Doctors and A S Ws should be ready to consult colleagues (especially C P Ns and other community care staff involved with the patient's care), while retaining for themselves the final responsibility. Where disagreements do occur, professionals should ensure that they have set out to each other in discussion their views of the salient features of the case and their conclusions.

2.29 Where there is an unresolved dispute about an application for admission, it is essential that the professionals do not abandon the patient and the family. Rather, they should explore and agree an alternative plan, if necessary on a temporary basis, and ensure that the family is kept informed. It is desirable for such a plan to be recorded in writing and copies made available to all those who need it (subject to the patient's right to confidentiality).

The choice of applicant

2.30 The A S W is usually the right applicant, bearing in mind professional training, knowledge of the legislation and of local resources, together with the potential adverse effect that a nearest relative application might have on the relationship with the patient. The doctor should therefore advise the nearest relative that it is preferable for an A S W to make an assessment of the need for a patient to be admitted under the Act, and for the A S W to make the application. When reasonably practicable the doctor should, however, advise the nearest relative of his section 13(4) rights (see para 2.33) and of his right to make an application.

2.31 The doctor should never advise the nearest relative to make an application in order to avoid involving an A S W in an assessment.

Agency responsibilities

The local authority

2.32 A nearest relative should not be forced to make an application himself for admission under the Act because it is not possible for an A S W to attend for assessment. Subject to resources, local authorities should aim to provide a 24 hour A S W service to ensure that this does not happen.

2.33 *Section 13(4)*. Local authorities should:

a. issue A S Ws with guidance on what amounts to a 'request' from a nearest relative;

b. have explicit policies on how to respond to repeated requests for assessment where the condition of a patient has not changed significantly;

c. give guidance to A S Ws as to whether nearest relative requests can be accepted by way of general practitioners (G Ps) or other professionals. (Such requests should certainly be accepted provided the G P or other professional has been so authorised by the nearest relative.)

Emergencies out of hours etc

2.34 Teams must pass on information to professional colleagues who are next on duty to enable them to make necessary arrangements; for example where an application for admission is not immediately necessary but might be in the future. For example, the necessary arrangements could then be made for an A S W to attend the next day.

Interpreters

2.35 Local and health authorities and N H S trusts should ensure that A S Ws and doctors receive sufficient guidance in the use of interpreters and should make arrangements for there to be an easily accessible pool of trained interpreters. Authorities and trusts should consider cooperating in making this provision. (See para 2.11(a) for further details.)

The health authority

Doctors approved under Section 12

2.36 The Secretary of State for Health has delegated to regional health authorities, and the Secretary of State for Wales to district health authorities, the task of approving medical practitioners under section 12(2).

2.37 Thus regional health authorities (in England) and district health authorities (in Wales) should:

a. take active steps to encourage sufficient doctors, including G Ps, to apply for approval;

b. seek to ensure a 24 hour on-call rota of approved doctors sufficient to cover the area;

c. maintain a regularly updated list of approved doctors which indicates how each approved doctor can be contacted and the hours that he is available;

d. ensure that the up-to-date list of approved doctors and details of the 24 hour on-call rota are circulated to all concerned parties including G Ps, mental health centres and social services.

2.38 Authorities and trusts should consider including in the job description for new consultant psychiatrists with a responsibility for providing a catchment area service obligations to become approved under section 12 of the Act, to keep such approval up-to-date and to participate in the 24 hour on-call approved doctors' rota.

Health authorities/N H S trusts/local authorities

2.39 Good practice requires that health authorities, N H S Trusts and local social services authorities should cooperate in ensuring that regular meetings take place between professionals involved in mental health assessment in order to promote understanding, and to provide a forum for clarification of their respective roles and responsibilities.

2.40 Authorities and N H S trusts should keep records of the ethnicity of all patients assessed under the Mental Health Act. They should ensure that they have a system to monitor equality of access to assessment by race and sex, and that assessments are free from social, cultural, racial, and gender bias.

3   Part III of the Mental Health Act – patients concerned with criminal proceedings

Assessment

General

Responsibility to patients

3.1 Those subject to criminal proceedings have the same right to psychiatric assessment and treatment as other citizens. The aim should be to ensure that everyone in prison or police custody in need of medical treatment for mental disorder which can only satisfactorily be given in a hospital as defined by the Act is admitted to such a hospital.

3.2 All professionals involved in the operation of Part III of the Act should remember:

a.   the vulnerability of people, especially those who are mentally disordered, when in police or prison custody. The risk of suicide or other self destructive behaviour should be of special concern;

b.   that a prison hospital is not a hospital within the meaning of the Act. Treatment facilities are limited, and the provisions of Part IV of the Act do not apply.

Individual professional responsibilities

3.3 All professionals concerned with the operation of Part III of the Act should be familiar with:

— the relevant provisions of the Act and paragraphs of the Memorandum (paras 115 to 188);

— any relevant guidance issued by or under the auspices of the Home Office including that in Home Office Circular 66/90 and E L(90)168, on Provision for Mentally Disordered Offenders;

— the responsibilities of their own and other disciplines and authorities and agencies;

— available facilities and services.

Agency responsibility

3.4 Regional health authorities in England and district health authorities in Wales should:

a. be able to provide to any requesting court in compliance with section 39 of the Act, and also in response to any other proper request, up-to-date and full information on the range of facilities for a potential patient in hospitals, including secure facilities. Facilities to which the patient might be admitted outside their district or region may need to be specified and the arrangements for their funding clarified;

b. appoint a named person to respond to these requests.

3.5 Section 27 of the Criminal Justice Act 1991 added a new section 39A to the Act which requires a local social services authority to inform the court if it or any other person is willing to receive the offender into guardianship and, if so, to provide such information as it reasonably can about how the guardian's powers can be expected to be exercised.

3.6 Local authorities should appoint a named person to respond to requests from the courts for them to consider the making of guardianship orders.

Assessment by a doctor

3.7 Where a doctor is asked to provide an opinion in relation to a possible admission under Part III of the Act:

a. he should identify himself to the person being assessed, and explain at whose request he is preparing his report, discussing any implications this may have for confidentiality;

b. he should have access to relevant social enquiry reports, the inmate's medical record (where the defendant is remanded in prison custody) and previous psychiatric treatment records as well as relevant documentation regarding the alleged offence. If he is not given any of this information he should say so clearly in his report (see paras 2.6 and 2.35).

Where a doctor had previously treated the person it may be desirable for him to prepare the report. It would also be desirable for the doctor (or one of them if two doctors are preparing reports) to have appropriate beds at his disposal or where necessary to take responsibility for referring the case to another doctor with access to such facilities.

3.8 The doctor should where possible make contact with independent information about the person's previous history, previous psychiatric treatment and patterns of behaviour.

3.9 Any assessment of the person is a medical responsibility. Appropriate members of the clinical team who would be involved with the individual's care and treatment may also be involved. It is often desirable for a nurse (who will be able to undertake a nursing assessment of the person's needs for nursing care and treatment and advise on whether he can be managed in the hospital) to accompany the assessing doctor where admission to hospital is likely to be recommended. The doctor should make contact with the social worker or probation officer who is preparing a social enquiry report, especially when psychiatric treatment is suggested as a condition of a probation order.

3.10 The doctor should not in his report anticipate the outcome of proceedings to establish guilt or innocence. It is sometimes appropriate to advise that a further report should be submitted to court after conviction and before sentencing. In any report prepared before a verdict is reached, the doctor may give advice on the appropriate disposal of the person in the event that he is convicted.

3.11 When the doctor has concluded that the person needs treatment in hospital, but there is no facility available, the task is not completed until:

a. details of the type of provision required have been forwarded in writing to the district health authority, who will need detailed advice in order to discharge their responsibilities;

b. in suitable cases contact has been made with the local N H S forensic psychiatrist.

Role of A S W

3.12 If an A S W has to be called to the prison or to a court to see a prisoner about to be released, with a view to making an application for admission as a detained patient under sections 2 or 3, as much advance warning as possible should be given, and the A S W must be given ample time and facilities for interviewing the prisoner. The A S W should be given access to the social inquiry report as it is difficult within the confines of a prison/court to assess how a prisoner (convicted or on remand) might be able to benefit from alternative treatment in the community.

Transfer of prisoners to hospital

3.13 The need for in-patient treatment for a prisoner must be identified and acted on swiftly, and contact made urgently between the prison doctor and the hospital doctor. The Home Office must be advised on the urgency of the need for transfer.

3.14 The transfer of a prisoner to hospital under the Act should not be delayed until close to his release date. A transfer in such circumstances may well be seen by the prisoner as being primarily intended to extend his detention and result in an unco-operative attitude towards treatment.

4 Private practice and the provision of medical recommendations

4.1 The Act restricts the provision of medical recommendations by certain categories of doctor in private practice. Thus:

a. where an individual is to be admitted to a mental nursing home or as a private patient to a hospital, neither medical recommendation can be provided by a doctor on the staff of the hospital or mental nursing home (section 12(3));

b. no medical recommendation can be provided by a doctor who receives, or has an interest in the receipt of, any payment made on account of the maintenance of the patient (section 12(5)(d)).

4.2 It is the personal responsibility of any doctor providing a medical recommendation to ensure that he is complying with these legal requirements; if in doubt legal advice must be sought.

4.3 It is undesirable for a doctor to provide a recommendation where he will receive payment from the patient (or a relative or friend or an insurance company) for his medical services after admission to hospital or a mental nursing home as a private patient.

4.4 If there could be any suspicion (however unjustified) that a doctor providing a medical recommendation is doing so for pecuniary advantage, then arrangements should be made for another doctor to do so.

4.5 Where the patient is currently receiving treatment from a doctor that doctor should be consulted by the doctor(s) providing the medical recommendation.

5 Section 2 or section 3

The choice

5.1 Which admission section should be used? Professional judgment must be applied to the criteria in each section and only when this has been done can a decision be reached as to which, if either, section applies. It must be borne in mind that detention under section 3 need not last any longer than under section 2.

5.2 **Section 2 pointers:**

a. where the diagnosis and prognosis of a patient's condition is unclear;

b. there is a need to carry out an in-patient assessment in order to formulate a treatment plan;

c. where a judgment is needed as to whether the patient will accept treatment on a voluntary basis following admission;

d. where a judgment has to be made as to whether a particular treatment proposal, which can only be administered to the patient under Part IV of the Act, is likely to be effective;

e. where a patient who has already been assessed, and who has been previously admitted compulsorily under the Act, is judged to have changed since the previous admission and needs further assessment;

f. where the patient has not previously been admitted to hospital either compulsorily or informally.

5.3 Section 3 pointers:

a. where a patient has been admitted in the past, is considered to need compulsory admission for the treatment of a mental disorder which is already known to his clinical team, and has been assessed in the recent past by that team;

b. where a patient already admitted under section 2 and who is assessed as needing further medical treatment for mental disorder under the Act at the conclusion of his detention under section 2 is unwilling to remain in hospital informally and to consent to the medical treatment;

c. where a patient is detained under section 2 and assessment points to a need for treatment under the Act for a period beyond the 28 day detention under section 2. In such circumstances an application for detention under section 3 should be made at the earliest opportunity and should not be delayed until the end of section 2 detention. Changing a patient's detention status from section 2 to section 3 will not deprive him of a Mental Health Review Tribunal hearing if the change takes place after a valid application has been made to the Tribunal but before it has been heard. The patient's rights to apply for a Tribunal under section 66(1)(b) in the first period of detention after his change of status are unaffected.

5.4 Decisions should **not** be influenced by:

a. wanting to avoid consulting the nearest relative;

b. the fact that a proposed treatment to be administered under the Act will last less than 28 days;

c. the fact that a patient detained under section 2 will get quicker access to a Mental Health Review Tribunal than one detained under section 3.

6 Admission for assessment in an emergency (section 4)

(Paras 28 and 29 of the Memorandum)

General

6.1 An applicant cannot seek admission for assessment under section 4 unless:

a. the criteria for admission for assessment are met, and

b. the matter is of urgent necessity and there is not enough time to get a second medical recommendation.

6.2 Section 4 is for use in a genuine emergency and should never be used for administrative convenience. Those involved in the process of admission are entitled to expect 'second doctors' to be available so that they do not have to consider using section 4 in circumstances other than genuine emergencies.

Admission

6.3 An emergency arises where those involved cannot cope with the mental state or behaviour of the patient. To be satisfied that an emergency has arisen, there must be evidence of:

—the existence of a significant risk of mental or physical harm to the patient or to others; and/or

—the danger of serious harm to property; and/or

—the need for physical restraint of the patient.

6.4 It is wrong for patients to be admitted under section 4 rather than section 2 because it is more convenient for the second doctor to examine the patient in, rather than outside, hospital. Those assessing an individual's need must be able to secure the attendance within a reasonable time of a second doctor and in particular an approved doctor.

6.5 If a 'second doctor' is not available to support an application under section 2, an application under section 4 cannot be made unless it is of urgent necessity.

6.6 If the A S W has no option but to consider an application for admission under section 4 and is not satisfied with the reasons for the non-availability of the second doctor he must:

a. discuss the case with the doctor providing the recommendation and seek to resolve the problem;

b. if this is not possible, and the A S W has to make an application for admission under section 4, have access to an officer in his local social services authority sufficiently senior to take up the matter with the health authority. The A S W's local authority should make it clear that the A S W in these circumstances is under an obligation to report the matter in this way.

6.7 The Managers should monitor the use of section 4 and seek to ensure the second doctors are available to visit a patient within a reasonable time after being so requested.

6.8 If a patient is admitted under section 4 an appropriate second doctor should examine him as soon as possible after admission, to decide whether the patient should be detained under section 2.

7 Part III of the Mental Health Act – patients concerned with criminal proceedings

Admission

From prison or remand centre

7.1 Where the receiving hospital does not already possess them the following must be sent at the time of the transfer:

—an up-to-date medical report (sent by the prison medical officer to the patient's responsible medical officer (r m o));

—any relevant social reports prepared by the probation service (addressed to the ward to which the patient has been admitted and marked for the attention of the relevant social worker or in his absence the patient's r m o).

It is important that all information is made available to the patient's r m o and other professional staff working with him.

Restricted patients

7.2 The Managers and the patient's r m o should ensure that where patients are admitted to hospital from prison under sections 47 or 48 the patients have received and, as far as possible, understood the letter from the Home Office explaining the role of the Managers and the r m o in relation to restricted patients.

Patients on remand/subject to an interim hospital order

7.3 For patients detained under sections 35, 36, 37 and 38 it is the court's responsibility to organise transport from the court to the receiving hospital. (See also para 28.6).

8 Doctor's holding power (section 5(2))

(Paras 30–32 of the Memorandum)

8.1 Good practice depends upon:

a. the professionals involved in its implementation (and in particular the doctor invoking the holding power) correctly understanding the power and its purpose;

b. the health authority/N H S trust/local social services authority making the necessary arrangements to ensure that when it is invoked the patient is fully assessed as speedily as possible by an A S W and doctors for a possible admission under the Act;

c. the Managers monitoring the use of the power.

Nature of the power

8.2 The power (which authorises the detention of the patient for up to 72 hours) can only be used where the doctor in charge (or his nominated deputy) of an in-patient's treatment (including in-patients being treated for physical disorders) concludes that an application for admission under the relevant sections of the Act is appropriate. The period of detention commences at the moment the doctor's report (form 12) is delivered to the Managers, or someone authorised to receive such a report on their behalf.

8.3 Any patient detained under section 5(2) should be discharged from the order immediately:

a. an assessment is carried out and a decision is taken not to make an application;

b. the doctor decides that no assessment for possible admission needs to be carried out.

The power cannot be renewed, but circumstances can arise where, subsequent to its use and the patient's reversion to informal status, its use can be considered again.

8.4 An informal in-patient, for the purpose of this section, is one who has understood and accepted the offer of a bed, who has freely appeared on the ward and who has co-operated in the admission procedure. The section, for example, cannot be used for an out-patient attending a hospital's accident and emergency department.

8.5 Where a report under section 5(2) is provided in relation to a patient under the care of a consultant other than a psychiatrist, the doctor invoking the power should make immediate contact with a psychiatrist.

8.6 Where a patient is receiving *treatment both for a physical disorder and a mental disorder*, in relation to section 5(2) the doctor in charge of treatment is the consultant psychiatrist concerned.

Information

8.7 Where a patient is detained under section 5(2), the Managers must ensure that the requirements of section 132 (information) are fulfilled.

Treatment

8.8 Part IV of the Act does not apply to a patient detained under section 5(2). In the absence of the patient's consent, therefore, treatment can only be given under the common law.

The doctor's role

8.9 Section 5(2) should only be invoked if the use of sections 2, 3 and 4 is not practicable or safe, i e section 5(2) is not an admission section under the Act.

8.10 The patient's doctor (or nominated deputy) must only use the power immediately after having personally examined the patient. No doctor should complete a section 5(2) form and leave it on the ward with instruction for others to submit it to the Managers if, in their view, the patient is about to leave.

8.11 The patient may only be detained when the doctor's section 5(2) report has been delivered to the Managers, or somebody authorized to receive it on their behalf (the doctor or nominated deputy must always be aware of who that person is).

Assessment for admission while a patient is 'held' under section 5(2)

8.12 All the normal rules apply, including the use of either section 2 or section 3 if compulsory admission is thought necessary.

Nominated deputies – section 5(3)

8.13 The registered medical practitioner in charge of an in-patient's treatment may nominate *one* deputy to exercise section 5(2) powers in his place during his absence from the hospital. That deputy will then act on his own responsibility and should be reasonably experienced.

8.14 **Some safeguards**

a. Where the nominated deputy is a junior doctor, the nominating doctor must be satisfied that his deputy has received sufficient guidance and training to carry out the function satisfactorily.

b. Wherever possible the nominated deputy must contact the nominating doctor or another consultant (where the nominated deputy is not a consultant) before using section 5(2). The nominated deputy should have easy access to the nominating doctor or the psychiatric consultant on-call.

c. Only registered medical practitioners who are consultant psychiatrists should nominate deputies.

d. The nominated deputy should report the use of section 5(2) to his nominator as soon as possible.

e. All relevant staff should know who is the nominated deputy for a particular patient.

8.15 *Remember*—it is unlawful for one nominated deputy to nominate another.

8.16 It is usual practice outside normal working hours for the nominated deputy to be the junior doctor on call for the admission wards, the junior doctors being on duty on a rota basis. Where this occurs the nominating doctor is responsible for ensuring that he is prepared to nominate all the doctors liable to be on duty and that they are adequately trained, and that he has nominated an individual doctor for every duty period. Where the duty rota is changed during a period of duty and a new doctor comes on call a change of nominated deputy must be agreed by the consultant in charge of the case or by the consultant on call.

9   The nurse's holding power (section 5(4))

(Paras 33–34 of the Memorandum)

The power

9.1 A psychiatric emergency is no different from any other medical emergency; it requires the urgent attendance of a doctor. In practice, a doctor may not be immediately available. This chapter sets out the circumstances in which a registered mental nurse or a registered nurse for the mentally handicapped (first level) may lawfully prevent an informal in-patient receiving medical treatment for mental disorder from leaving the hospital – for up to 6 hours or until a doctor with the power to use section 5(2) in respect of the patient arrives, whichever is the earlier. It is the personal decision of the nurse and he cannot be instructed to exercise this power by anyone else. Part IV of the Mental Health Act does not apply to patients detained under section 5(4).

Assessment before implementation

9.2 Before using the power the nurse should assess:

a.   the likely arrival time of the doctor as against the likely intention of the patient to leave. Most patients who express a wish to leave hospital can be persuaded to wait until a doctor arrives to discuss it further. Where this is not possible the nurse must try to predict the impact of any delay upon the patient;

b.   the consequences of a patient leaving hospital immediately – the harm that might occur to the patient or others – taking into account:

— what the patient says he will do;

— the likelihood of the patient committing suicide;

— the patient's current behaviour and in particular any changes in usual behaviour;

— the likelihood of the patient behaving in a violent manner;

— any recently received messages from relatives or friends;

— any recent disturbance on the ward (which may or may not involve the patient);

— any relevant involvement of other patients.

c. the patient's known unpredictability and any other relevant information from other members of the multi-disciplinary team.

Acute emergencies

9.3 Normally assessment should precede action but in extreme circumstances it may be necessary to invoke the power without carrying out the proper assessment. The suddenness of the patient's determination to leave and the urgency with which the patient attempts to do so should alert the nurse to potentially serious consequences if the patient is successful in leaving.

Reports

9.4 The nurse (who must be entitled to use the power) invokes it by completing form 13. This must be delivered to the Managers (or an officer appointed by them) as soon as possible after completion. It is essential that:

a. the reasons for invoking the power are entered in the patient's nursing and medical notes;

b. a local incident report form is sent to the Managers.

9.5 At the time the power elapses the nurse must complete form 16.

Use of restraint

9.6 A nurse invoking section 5(4) is entitled to use the minimum force necessary to prevent the patient from leaving hospital. The general principles that should be applied when the use of restraint has to be considered are set out in paras 18.6 and 18.7.

9.7 The nurse in charge of the ward should explain in private to the patient the need for using section 5(4) and, when it occurs, the need to lock the ward door.

Management responsibilities

9.8 The use of section 5(4) is an emergency measure and the doctor with the power to use section 5(2) in respect of the patient should treat it as such, arriving as soon as possible. The doctor must not wait six hours before attending simply because this is the maximum time allowed. If the doctor has not arrived within four hours the duty consultant should be contacted and should attend. Where no doctor has attended within six hours an oral report (suitably recorded) should be made immediately to the unit general manager or the equivalent officer in a N H S trust, and a written report should be submitted to the unit general manager or the equivalent officer in a N H S trust and the Managers on the next working day. The unit general manager or the equivalent officer in a N H S trust should nominate a suitable person to supervise the patient's leaving.

9.9 The holding power lapses upon the arrival of the doctor.

9.10 A suitably qualified nurse should be on all wards where there is a possibility of section 5(4) being invoked. Although the section is more likely to have to be used on acute admission wards, and wards where there are acutely disturbed patients, or patients requiring intensive nursing care, local management must also assess the potential for its use elsewhere in the hospital or unit. As a result of such assessment they should ensure that suitable arrangements are in place for a suitably qualified nurse to be available should the power need to be invoked.

10 The police power to remove to a place of safety (section 136)

(Para 293 of the Memorandum)

Good practice

10.1 This depends on:

a. the local social services authority, district health authority, N H S trust and the Chief Officer of Police establishing a clear policy for its implementation;

b. all professionals involved in its implementation understanding the power and its purpose and following the local policy concerning its implementation.

The local policy

10.2 The aim of the policy should be to secure the competent and speedy assessment by a doctor *and* an A S W of the person detained under the power.

10.3 The policy should define, in particular, the responsibilities of:

a. police officers to remain in attendance, where the patient's health or safety or the protection of others so require when the patient is taken to a place of safety (other than a police station);

b. police officers, doctors and A S Ws for the satisfactory returning to the community of a person assessed under section 136 who is not admitted to hospital or immediately placed in accommodation.

10.4 The policy should include provisions for the use of the section to be monitored so that:

a.   a check can be made of how and in what circumstances it is being used, including its use in relation to given categories of people, such as those from particular ethnic or cultural groups;

b.   informed consideration can be given by all parties to the policy to any changes in the mental health services that might result in the reduction of its use.

The place of safety

10.5 The identification of preferred places of safety is a matter for local agreement. Regard should be had to any impact different types of place of safety may have on the person held and hence on the outcome of an assessment.

Good practice points

10.6 Where an individual is detained by the police under section 136 it is desirable that:

a.   where he is to be taken to a hospital as a place of safety *immediate* contact is made by the police with both the hospital and the local social services department;

b.   where the police station is to be used as a place of safety immediate contact is made with the local social services authority and the appropriate doctor.

The local policy for the implementation of section 136 should ensure that police officers have no difficulty in identifying whom to contact.

Record keeping

10.7 A record of the person's time of arrival must be made immediately he reaches the place of safety. As soon as the individual is no longer detained under section 136 he must be so advised by those who are detaining him. It would be good practice for Managers (where the hospital is used as the place of safety) to devise and use a form for recording the end of the person's detention under this section (similar to the form used for section 5(4)).

10.8 Section 136 is not an emergency admission section. It enables an individual who falls within its criteria to be detained for the purposes of an assessment by a doctor and A S W, and for any necessary arrangements for his treatment and care to be made. When these have been completed within the 72 hour detention period, the authority to detain the patient ceases. Where a hospital is used as a place of safety it may be better for the patient not to be formally admitted although he may have to be cared for on a ward. Where such a policy is adopted it is essential to remember that the patient must be examined by a doctor in the same way as if he had been formally admitted.

Information about rights

10.9 Where an individual has been removed to a place of safety by the police under section 136:

a.   the person removed is entitled to have another person of his choice informed of his removal and his whereabouts (section 56 of the Police and Criminal Evidence Act 1984);

b.   when the person removed is in police detention (that is, a police station is being used as a place of safety) he has a right of access to legal advice (section 58 of the Police and Criminal Evidence Act 1984).

c.   where detention is in a place of safety other than a police station access to legal advice should be facilitated whenever it is requested.

It is important to recognise that although the Act uses the term 'remove', it is deemed to be an 'arrest' for the purposes of the Police and Criminal Evidence Act 1984.

10.10 Where the hospital is used as a place of safety the Managers must ensure that the provisions of section 132 (information) are complied with.

10.11 Where the police station is a place of safety, although section 132 does not apply, it would be good practice for the policy referred to above to require that the same information is given in writing on the person's arrival at the place of safety.

Assessment

10.12 The local implementation policy should ensure that the doctor examining the patient should wherever possible be 'approved'.

10.13 Assessment by both doctor and social worker should begin as soon as possilbe after the arrival of the individual at the place of safety. Any implementation policy should set target times for the commencement of the assessment and the health authority/N H S trust/local authority should review what happens in practice against these targets.

10.14 The person must be seen by *both* the doctor and the A S W. The local policy should include the necessary arrangements to enable the person wherever possible to be jointly assessed. If the doctor sees the person first and concludes that admission to hospital is unnecessary, or the person agrees to informal admission, the individual must still be seen by an A S W, who must consult with the doctor about any other necessary arrangements for his treatment and care that might need to be made. It is desirable for a consultant psychiatrist in learning disabilities (mental handicap) and an A S W with experience of working with people with learning disabilities to be available to make a joint assessment should there be a possibility that the detained person has a learning disability.

10.15 The role of the A S W includes:

- interviewing the person;
- contacting any relevant relatives/friends;
- ascertaining whether there is a psychiatric history;
- considering any possible alternatives to admission to hospital;
- considering the need to make any other 'necessary' arrangements.

Treatment

10.16 Part IV of the Act does not apply to persons detained under section 136. In the absence of consent the person can only be treated in accordance with the provisions of the common law. (see Chapter 15)

Necessary arrangements

10.17 Once the assessment has been concluded it is the responsibility of the doctors and A S W to consider if any necessary arrangements for the person's treatment and care have to be made.

10.18 Where compulsory admission is indicated:

a. where the hospital is the place of safety the person should be admitted either under section 2 or section 3 (whichever is appropriate). Wherever possible where the approved doctor providing one recommendation is on the staff of the hospital (as is usually the case) the second recommendation should be provided by a doctor with previous knowledge of the person (for example his G P). It has to be recognised that many people detained under section 136 are not registered with a G P and in these circumstances as well as where it is not possible to secure the attendance of a G P who knows the person, it would be preferable for the second opinion to be provided by a second approved doctor;

b. persons detained under section 136 in hospital pending completion of their assessment should not find their detention being continued under section 5(2) or section 5(4);

c. where the police station is the place of safety then compulsory admission should be under section 2 or 3 (whichever is appropriate); but there may be exceptional circumstances where there is urgent necessity to remove the person to hospital, in which case section 4 must be considered.

10.19 Section 136 provides the lawful authority for the removal by the police of a person to whom the provision applies from a place to which the public have access. Where it is necessary to consider gaining access to (and possibly removing to a place of safety) a mentally disordered individual other than in a public place and where access is denied then consideration must be given to invoking the powers of entry under section 135(1) or (2). Local authorities should issue guidance to A S Ws on how to invoke the power.

11 Conveying to hospital

(Para 36 of the Memorandum)

General

11.1 Where an A S W is the applicant he has a professional responsibility for ensuring that all the necessary arrangements are made for the patient to be conveyed to hospital.

11.2 Where the nearest relative is the applicant, the assistance of an A S W is recommended and should be made available if requested. If this is not possible, other professionals involved in the admission should be prepared to give advice and assistance.

11.3 Authorities (including the ambulance service and the police) likely to be involved in conveying patients to hospital should prepare and publish joint policy/procedures to include:

a. a clear statement of the roles and obligations of each authority and its personnel;

b. the form of any authorisation to be given by the A S W to others to convey the patient to hospital;

c. guidance to personnel as to their powers in relation to conveying patients to hospital.

The local authority should take the lead in producing such guidance.

The Approved Social Worker

11.4 Where the approved social worker is the applicant he has a professional obligation to consider and then implement the most humane and least threatening method of conveying the patient consistent with ensuring that no harm comes to the patient or to others. He should ensure that the needs of the patient are not overlooked while trying to ensure that the legalities are observed. He should take into account:

- the patient's wishes;
- the views of concerned relatives or friends involved with his admission;
- the views of other professionals involved in the application or who know the patient;
- his judgement of the patient's state of mind, and the likelihood of the patient behaving in a violent or dangerous manner;
- the impact that any particular mode of conveying the patient will have on the patient's relationship with the community to which he will return.

11.5 The A S W is permitted to delegate the task of conveying the patient to another person (e g ambulance personnel or possibly the police). But the A S W retains ultimate responsibility to ensure that the patient is conveyed in a lawful and humane manner, and must be ready to give the necessary guidance to those asked to assist.

11.6 It will often be best to convey the patient by ambulance; the A S W will need to decide if he should accompany the patient. Where requested by the applicant, the ambulance authority should be willing to make the necessary arrangements. If the patient would prefer to be accompanied by another professional (perhaps better known to him) or by a responsible relative, the A S W may ask that person to escort the patient, provided he is satisfied that he in doing so he is not increasing the risk of harm to the patient or others.

11.7 The patient should not be conveyed to hospital by car unless the A S W is satisfied the patient will not be a danger to himself or others. There should *always* be an escort for the patient other than the driver.

11.8 If the patient is likely to be violent or dangerous the police should be asked to help. Such a patient should never be conveyed by car. Where possible an ambulance should be used. Otherwise a police vehicle suitable for conveying such a patient should be used. While the police may have to exercise their duty to protect persons or property while the patient is being conveyed they should, where this is not inconsistent with their duty, comply with any directions or guidance given by the A S W.

11.9 The A S W should telephone the receiving hospital to ensure that the patient is expected and give the likely time of arrival. If possible he should ask the name of the person who will be formally receiving the admission documents.

11.10 The A S W must ensure that the admission documents arrive at the receiving hospital at the same time as the patient. If the A S W is not travelling in the same vehicle as the patient, the documents should be given to the person authorised to convey the patient with instructions for them to be presented to the officer authorised to receive them.

11.11 If the A S W is not travelling with the patient, he should arrive at the hospital at the same time or as soon as possible afterwards. He should ensure that the admission documents have been delivered, that the admission of the patient is under way and that any relevant information in his possession is passed to appropriate personnel in the hospital. He should remain in the hospital with the patient until he is satisfied that the patient has been detained in a proper manner.

11.12 A patient who has been sedated before being conveyed to hospital should whenever possible be accompanied by a nurse, a doctor or a suitably trained ambulance person experienced in the management of such patients.

12 Receipt and scrutiny of documents

(Paras 50–55 of the Memorandum)

12.1 The Managers should formally delegate their duties to receive and scrutinise admission documents to a limited number of officers with an adequate knowledge of the relevant parts of the Act. There must be adequate 24 hour cover. It is best that a general manager should take overall responsibility on behalf of the Managers for the proper receipt and scrutiny of documents.

12.2 There is a difference between 'receiving' documents and 'scrutinising' them. Although it is desirable that documents should be scrutinised at the same time as they are received, circumstances will often dictate that in order for it to be done properly scrutiny should take place later.

Receipt of documents

12.3 Some guiding rules:

a. where the Managers' obligation to receive documents is delegated to nursing staff, such delegation should be to the nurse in charge of the ward. If the nurse is below the grade of first level nurse, he should seek the advice of a first level nurse when 'receiving' documents;

b. the hospital should have a check list for the guidance of those delegated to receive documents, to ensure that they do not contain any errors which cannot be corrected at a later stage in the procedure (see section 15);

c. when the patient is being admitted on the application of an A S W the person 'receiving' the admission documents should check their accuracy with the A S W;

d. the 'receiving' officer should have access to a manager for advice, especially at night.

41

'Scrutinising' documents

12.4 Some guiding rules:

a. where the person delegated to receive the documents is not authorised by the Managers to rectify a defective admission document the documents must be scrutinised by a person so authorised immediately on the patient's admission (or during the next working day if the patient is admitted at night, weekends or public holidays when such a person is not available);

b. the Managers must arrange for the medical recommendations to be medically scrutinised, to ensure that they show sufficient legal grounds for detention. The clinical description of the patient's mental condition should include a description of his symptoms and of his behaviour, not merely a diagnostic classification. This scrutiny should be carried out at the same time as the administrative scrutiny (see immediately above).

Managers

12.5 Some guiding rules:

a. the Managers are responsible for ensuring that patients are detained lawfully; they should therefore monitor the receipt and scrutiny of admission documents on a regular basis;

b. those delegated to scrutinise documents must be clear about what kinds of errors on application forms and medical recommendations can and cannot be corrected (see paras 52–55 of the Memorandum). If no original pink forms are available photocopies of an original form can be used;

c. details of defective admission documents, whether rectifiable or not, and of any subsequent action, must be given to the Managers on a regular basis;

d. Managers should ensure that those delegated to receive and scrutinise admission documents understand the requirements of the Act, and if necessary receive appropriate training.

13   Guardianship (section 7)

(Paras 43–48 of the Memorandum)

Purpose of guardianship

13.1 The purpose of guardianship is to enable patients to receive community care where it cannot be provided without the use of compulsory powers. It enables the establishment of an authoritative framework for working with a patient with a miminum of constraint to achieve as independent as life as possible within the community. Where it is used it must be part of the patient's overall care and treatment plan.

Assessment for guardianship

13.2 A S W's and registered medical practitioners should consider guardianship as a positive alternative when making decisions about a patient's treatment and welfare. In particular it should be actively considered as an alternative both to admission to hospital and to continuing hospital care.

13.3 Any application for guardianship should be based on discussions among most professionals who are or who could be involved in the patient's care, and the A S W assessing the needs and appropriateness of guardianship. This should be by way of a multi-disciplinary case discussion, but if guardianship is to be considered as an alternative to admission it may not be possible to arrange such a meeting in the time available. It is important that any procedures instituted by social services departments are no more than the minimum necessary to ensure the proper use of guardianship and that guardianship can be used in a positive and flexible manner. Any application for guardianship should be accompanied by a comprehensive care plan established on the basis of multi-disciplinary discussions.

Components of effective guardianship

13.4 A comprehensive care plan is required which identifies the services needed by the patient, including as necessary his care arrangements, appropriate accommodation, his treatment and personal support requirements and those who have responsibilities under the care plan. The care plan should indicate which of the powers given by the guardianship order are necessary to achieve the plan. If no power is considered necessary for achieving any part of the care plan guardianship is inappropriate.

13.5 There will need to be the following components:

a. a recognition by the patient of the 'authority' of the guardian. There must be a willingness on the part of both parties to work together within the terms of the authority which is vested in the guardian by the Act;

b. the guardian should be willing to 'advocate' on behalf of the patient in relation to those agencies whose services are needed to carry out the care plan;

c. readily available support from the local authority for the guardian;

d. an appropriate place of residence taking into account the patient's needs for support, care, treatment and protection;

e. access to necessary day care, education and training facilities;

f. effective cooperation and communication between all persons concerned in implementing the care plan;

g. commitment on the part of all concerned that care should take place in the community.

Duty of social services department

13.6 Each local authority should prepare and publish a policy setting out the arrangements for:

a. receiving, considering and scrutinising applications for guardianship. Such arrangements should ensure that applications are adequately, but *speedily*, considered;

b. monitoring the progress of the guardianship including steps to be taken to fulfil the authority's statutory obligations in relation to private guardians and to arrange visits to the patient;

c. ensuring the suitability of any proposed private guardian and that the private guardian understand and carry out his statutory duties, including the appointment of a nominated medical attendant;

d. ensuring that the patients under guardianship receive, both orally and in writing, relevant aspects of the same information that health authorities are required to give to detained patients under section 132;

e. ensuring, in particular, that the patient is aware of his right to apply to a Mental Health Review Tribunal and that a named officer of the local authority will give any necessary assistance to the patient in making such an application;

f. maintaining detailed records relating to the person under guardianship;

g. ensuring the review of the patient's detention under guardianship towards the end of each period of detention;

h. discharging the guardianship order rather than allowing it to lapse.

The powers of the guardian

13.7 Section 8 of the Act sets out the three powers of the guardian as follows:

a. to require the patient to live at a place specified by the guardian. This does not provide the legal authority to detain a patient physically in such a place, nor does it authorise the removal of a patient against his wish. If the patient is absent without leave from the specified place he may be returned within 28 days by those authorised to do so under the Act;

b. to require the patient to attend at specified places for medical treatment, occupation, education or training. If the patient refuses to attend the guardian is not authorised to use force to secure such attendance, nor does the Act enable medical treatment to be administered in the absence of the patient's consent;

c. to require access to the patient to be given at the place where he is living to persons detailed in the Act. A refusal without reasonable cause to permit an authorised person to have access to the patient is an offence under section 129. Neither the guardian nor any authorised person can use force to secure entry. If the patient consistently resists the exercise of the guardian's powers it can be concluded that guardianship is not the most appropriate form of care for that person and the guardianship order should be discharged.

13.8 Points to remember:

a. guardianship does not restrict the patient's access to hospital services on a voluntary basis. If the patient should require treatment and there is no need to detain for treatment, he may be admitted informally and may remain under guardianship unless discharged or transferred;

b. the guardianship order can also remain in force if the patient is admitted to hospital under sections 2 or 4. It does not remain in force if the patient is admitted for treatment under section 3;

c. it is possible in certain circumstances for a patient liable to be detained in hospital by virtue of an application under Part II of the Act to be transferred into guardianship and for a person subject under Part II of the Act to be transferred into the guardianship of another local social services authority or person approved by such authority or to be transferred to hospital. (See section 19 and rules 7–9 of the Mental Health (Hospital, Guardianship and Consent to Treatment) Regulations 1983.)

13.9 Particular practice issues:

a. guardianship must not be used to require a patient to reside in hospital save in very exceptional circumstances where it is necessary for a very short time in order to provide shelter whilst a place of residence in the community is being obtained;

b. where an adult is assessed as requiring residential care but owing to mental incapacity is unable to make a decision as to whether he wishes to be placed in residential care, those who are responsible for his care should consider the applicability and appropriateness of guardianship for providing a framework within which decisions about his current and future care can be planned. Guardianship should never be used solely for the purpose of transferring any unwilling person into residential care.

Guardianship under section 37

13.10 As a potentially useful alternative to hospital orders, courts are empowered to make guardianship orders where the prescribed criteria, which are similar to those of a hospital order, are met and the court having regard to all the circumstances considers reception into the guardianship of the local services authority, or of any other person, appropriate. Guardianship orders may be particularly suitable in helping to meet the needs of mentally impaired offenders who could benefit from occupation, training and education in the community. Before making such an order the court has to be satisfied that the local authority or person is willing to act as guardian. The local authority will need to be satisfied with the arrangements and in considering the appropriateness of guardianship they will be guided by the same principles as apply under Part II of the Act. Similarly the powers and duties conferred on the local authority or private guardian and the provisions as to duration, renewal and discharge are those which apply to guardianship applications except that the power to discharge is not available to the nearest relative.

14 Information

(Paras 274–278 of the Memorandum)

General

14.1 All patients should be given, throughout their stay in hospital, as much information as possible about their care and treatment. Additionally it should be made clear to informal patients that they are allowed to leave hospital at any time. Subject to the requirements of the Act, information should be given in a suitable manner and at a suitable time to ensure that the patient understands as much as possible. Requests for information from the patient should be encouraged and answered honestly and comprehensively. Periodic checks should be made to ensure that patients continue to understand the information given to them. The purpose of information is to help people understand why they are in hospital. In particular it is important that informal patients understand their right to leave hospital. The Department of Health publishes leaflets about the information required to be given under section 132.

14.2 Information for patients must be displayed on ward notice boards, in reception areas and in any other suitable areas. Admission booklets should fully explain all essential matters concerning care and treatment. They should also refer to the availability of the leaflets describing the work and membership of the Mental Health Act Commission. A complaints leaflet should provide specific information as provided for in Circular HC(88)37 including the fact that hospital Managers monitor the handling of complaints. Health authorities and trusts should make arrangements with the local authority to maintain similar publicity in hospital premises of the social services department complaints procedures.

Statutory information

14.3 Section 132 requires the Managers to take all practical steps to ensure that *all* detained patients are given and understand:

a. specific information as soon as is practicable after their admission (see section 132 and para 274 of the Memorandum);

b. particular information insofar as it is relevant to the patient (see section 132(2) and para 275 of the Memorandum).

14.4 The Managers are also required to ensure that the above information is given in writing to the patient's nearest relative – unless the patient wishes otherwise. Health authorities and trusts are reminded that draft letters to nearest relatives were circulated at Annex B of Circular HC(83)17.

14.5 Section 133 requires that (unless the patient objects) the nearest relative should, if practicable, be given at least seven days notice of a detained patient's discharge from hospital or mental nursing home, especially if he is going to be involved in the aftercare of the patient.

The Managers' information policy

14.6 In carrying out their statutory responsibilities the Managers will need to devise a system which ensures that:

a. the right information is given to the patient;

b. the information is given in a suitable manner and at a suitable time in accordance with the requirements of the law;

c. the person who is to give the information is identified in relation to each detained patient. The Managers will need to ensure that staff know what information is to be given and that they have received sufficient training and guidance to enable them to give it;

d. a record is kept of the information given;

e. a check is made that information has been properly given to each detained patient.

14.7 The Managers should ensure that a member of staff is designated to check the patient's records regularly to ensure that all information has been given at the appropriate times, and that it has been repeated as necessary. This officer should also be available to give advice to those whose job it is to give information.

14.8 As far as practicable, the Managers (if appropriate in co-operation with the relevant local authorities) should ensure that an interpreter service is set up which, in addition to making use of interpreters in the community, would invite staff members with appropriate language skills to offer their assistance, and make appropriate training available to them.

Who should give the information

14.9 The Managers will need to delegate someone within the patient's multi-disciplinary team to give the information. This should be a flexible arrangement; for example, there will be cases where a patient may have a special rapport with a particular member of staff to whom the task could be delegated. But the Managers retain the ultimate responsibility for complying with the statutory requirements.

Patients with hearing impairment

14.10 The information giver should seek the assistance of a local authority or voluntary agency social worker for the deaf. In case of difficulties the advice of the British Deaf Association or the Royal National Institute for the Deaf should be sought.

Patients with visual impairment

14.11 The statutory information should be made available to them either in braille (where appropriate) or on tape. In the case of difficulties the Royal National Institute for the Blind should be asked for advice.

Recording

14.12 The person giving the advice should record on the patients' case notes all details about the information given, the various attempts to give it, patients' reactions, and an assessment of their comprehension at every stage in the procedure. This will not only serve as a record of compliance with the requirements of section 132 but also as an aide-memoire for staff.

Particular information

14.13 Certain events which will arise in the course of the patient's stay in hospital will need to be appropriately explained. Some of them are set out below:

a. *Consent to treatment.* The patient must be informed, in terms which he is likely to understand, of the nature, purpose and likely effects of the treatment proposed. (See Chapters 15 and 16). Patients must be advised of their rights to withdraw consent to treatment at any time before its completion and of the need for them to give fresh consent to treatment thereafter. If relevant a detained patient should be told how his refusal or withdrawal of consent can be over-ridden by the second opinion process operated by the Mental Health Act Commission and, where treatment has begun, of the doctor's power to continue it on an urgent basis if the discontinuance would cause serious suffering to the patient. (These explanations should be the responsibility of medical and nursing staff.)

b. *Renewal of detention and transfer to informal status.* A patient may need to be told of the provision in the Act under which he is detained and of its effect; care should be taken to ensure that the patient does not assume that he will be discharged on expiry of the current detention period nor that his detention will automatically be renewed. All future possibilities and options should be explained as early as possible. When the Managers are considering the renewal of a patient's detention, the patient should be told that he has a right to be heard by them, and advised how he may exercise this right. Administrative staff should be responsible for these explanations. The patient should also be advised of his right to ask the Managers to consider his discharge.

c. *Applications to Mental Health Review Tribunals.* There is a statutory obligation on the Managers to tell a detained patient of his right to apply to a Mental Health Review Tribunal. In addition, Managers should regard it as an obligation to ensure that patients and their nearest relatives know of the existence and role of these tribunals and of their respective rights of application to them. The Managers should ensure that patients remain aware of their rights to apply to a tribunal and are given every opportunity and assistance to exercise those rights, including facilities for representation. The patient should be told of his right to be represented by a lawyer of his choice and about the Law Society's Mental Health Review Tribunal representation panel list and other appropriate organisations, and should be given every assistance in using any of them. Managers should designate a member of staff to see personally every detained patient who applies to a tribunal or who is referred to a tribunal and to give them every reasonable assistance in securing representation (if the patient wishes).

d. *The Mental Health Act Commission.* There is a statutory obligation to advise patients about the Mental Health Act Commission. In addition patients should be made aware of visits made by the Commissioners to hospitals and of the opportunities which they will then have to meet the Commissioners. The Managers should also ensure that detained patients know that they have a right to complain to the Commission about their detention, treatment or general care, if they are not satisfied with the investigation of a complaint made to the Managers. Notices of visits of the Mental Health Act Commission should be prominently displayed and individual patients notified wherever possible.

e. *Other information.* Information-givers must bear in mind the need to give other information which could assist the patient, for example, the name of his r m o, the name of the member of the general manager's staff to whom he can turn, how to complain and, as far as Part III patients are concerned, the possibility of considering an appeal against the sentence.

15   Medical treatment

(Paras 189–205 of the Memorandum)

Introduction

15.1 This chapter, whilst referring to some aspects of the Mental Health Act, is primarily concerned with medical treatment generally and in particular capacity (see paras 15.9–15.11) and consent to treatment (see paras 15.12–15.24).

15.2 Everyone involved in the medical treatment of mental disorder should be familiar with the provisions of Part IV of the Act, related statutory instruments, relevant circulars and advice notes. But it is for the r m o to ensure that there is compliance with the Act's provisions relating to medical treatment.

15.3 The Managers should arrange to monitor compliance with the provisions of Part IV of the Act. (For a more detailed discussion of Part IV of the Act see Chapter 16).

Medical treatment

15.4 For the purposes of the Act, medical treatment includes 'nursing and also includes care, habilation and rehabilitation under medical supervision', i e the broad range of activities aimed at alleviating, or preventing a deterioration of, the patient's mental disorder. It includes physical treatment such as E C T and the administration of drugs, and psychotherapy.

Treatment plans

15.5 Treatment plans are essential for both informal and detained patients. Consultants should co-ordinate the formulation of a treatment plan in consultation with their professional colleagues. The plan should be recorded in the patient's clinical notes.

15.6 A treatment plan should include a description of the immediate and long-term goals for the patient with a clear indication of the treatments proposed and the methods of treatment. The patient's progress and possible changes to the plan should be reviewed at regular intervals.

15.7 Wherever possible the whole plan should be discussed with the patient, with a view to him making his own contribution and saying whether or not he agrees with it. It is also important to discuss it with the appropriate relatives concerned about a patient (but only with his consent in cases where the patient is capable of providing consent).

Capacity and consent to treatment: introduction

15.8 In general the common law, as it relates to consent to treatment, applies to all patients, informal or detained. Therefore, valid consent is required from a patient before medical treatment can be given, except where the law (either the common law or statute) provides authority to treat him without consent. The common law may authorise treatment where the patient is incapable of consenting (see paras 15.9–15.11 and 15.16–15.23) or, rarely, even where the patient can consent (see, for one set of circumstances, para 15.24). Statute law may authorise treatment, for example Part IV of the Act (see Chapter 16).

Capacity to make treatment decisions

15.9 The assessment of a patient's capacity to make a decision about his own medical treatment is a matter for clinical judgment, guided by current professional practice and subject to legal requirements. It is the personal responsibility of any doctor proposing to treat a patient to determine whether the patient has capacity to give a valid consent.

Capacity: the basic principles

15.10 An individual in order to have capacity must be able to:

- understand what medical treatment is and that somebody has said that he needs it and why the treatment is being proposed;

- understand in broad terms the nature of the proposed treatment;

- understand its principal benefits and risks;

- understand what will be the consequences of not receiving the proposed treatment;

- possess the capacity to make a choice.

It must be remembered:

- any assessment as to an individual's capacity has to be made in relation to a particular treatment proposal;

- capacity in an individual with a mental disorder can be variable over time and should be assessed at the time the treatment is proposed;

- all assessments of an individual's capacity should be fully recorded in the patient's medical notes.

15.11 A person suffering from a mental disorder is not necessarily incapable of giving consent. Capacity to consent is variable in people with mental disorder and should be assessed in relation to the particular patient, at the particular time, as regards the particular treatment proposed. Not everyone is equally capable of understanding the same explanation of a treatment plan. A person is more likely to be able to give valid consent if the explanation is appropriate to the level of his assessed ability.

Consent; the basic principles

15.12 'Consent' is the voluntary and continuing permission of the patient to receive a particular treatment, based on an adequate knowledge of the purpose, nature, likely effects and risks of that treatment including the likelihood of its success and any alternatives to it. Permission given under any unfair or undue pressure is not 'consent'.

Consent from patients with capacity to consent

15.13 The information which must be given should be related to the particular patient, the particular treatment and the relevant medical knowledge and practice. In every case sufficient information must be given to ensure that the patient understands in broad terms the nature, likely effects and risks of that treatment including the likelihood of its success and any alternatives to it. Additional information is a matter of professional judgement for the doctor proposing the treatment. The patient should be invited to ask questions and the doctor should answer fully, frankly, and truthfully. There may be a compelling reason, in the patient's interest, for not disclosing certain information. A doctor who chooses not to disclose must be prepared to justify the decision. If a doctor chooses not to answer a patient's question, he should make this clear so that the patient knows where he stands.

15.14 The patient should be told that his consent to treatment can be withdrawn at any time and that fresh consent is required before further treatment can be given or reinstated. The patient should receive an explanation of the likely consequences of not receiving treatment. (See para 16.15 on withdrawing consent in relation to treatment administered under Part IV of the Act.)

15.15 It is the duty of everyone proposing to give treatment to use reasonable care and skill, not only in giving information prior to seeking a patient's consent but also in meeting the continuing obligation to provide the patient with adequate information about the proposed treatment and alternatives to it.

Treatment of those without capacity to consent

15.16 There are three instances in which a patient who is not capable of giving consent may be treated, which are dealt with in the following paragraphs.

15.17 A patient may be incapable of giving consent because he is an immature child, in which case a parent or person with parental responsibility may consent (see Chapter 30).

15.18 A patient can be given treatment without consent when he is incapable of giving consent because he is unconscious and is in urgent need of treatment to preserve life, health or well-being (unless there is unequivocal and reliable evidence that the patient did not want that treatment), provided that it is necessary that the treatment be administered while the patient is still unconscious.

15.19 A patient can be given treatment without consent when he is incapable of giving consent provided two conditions are satisfied. The first condition is that the patient must lack the capacity (see paras 15.10 and 15.11) to make a decision and be in need of medical care. The second condition is that the treatment must be 'in the patient's best interests', which, according to the decision of the House of Lords in *Re F* [1990] 2 A C 1, means that the treatment is:

- necessary to save life or prevent a deterioration or ensure an improvement in the patient's physical or mental health; and

- in accordance with a practice accepted at the time by a responsible body of medical opinion skilled in the particular form of treatment in question (the test that was originally laid down in *Bolam v Friern Hospital Management Committee* [1957] 1 W L R 582).

There are exceptional circumstances in which the proposed treatment should not be carried out on incapable patients without first seeking the approval of the High Court by way of a declaration (see para 15.21). Sterilisation, according to the House of Lords in *Re F* (1990), is one such circumstance.

15.20 The administration of medical treatment to people incapable of taking their own treatment decisions is a matter of much concern to professionals and others involved in their care. It is the personal responsibility of professionals to ensure that they understand the relevant law.

15.21 The procedures to be used when applying for a declaration that a proposed operation for sterilisation is lawful were set out initially by Lord Brandon of Oakbrook in *Re F* and developed by the Official Solicitor in *Practice Note (Official Solicitor: Sterilisation)* [1990] 2 F L R 530. In outline, the procedure is as follows:

i. applications for a declaration that a proposed operation on or medical treatment for a patient can lawfully be carried out despite the inability of such patient to consent thereto should be by way of Originating Summons issuing out of the Family Division of the High Court;

ii. the applicant should normally be the person(s) responsible for the care of the patient or intending to carry out the proposed operation or other treatment, if it is declared to be lawful;

iii. the patient must always be a party and should normally be a respondent. In cases in which the patient is a respondent the patient's guardian ad litem should normally be the Official Solicitor. In any cases in which the Official Solicitor is not either the next friend or the guardian ad litem of the patient or an applicant he shall be respondent;

iv. with a view to protecting the patient's privacy, but subject always to the judge's discretion, the hearing will be in chambers, but the decision and the reasons for that decision will be given in court.

15.22 The *Handbook of Contraceptive Practice* (1990) considers the effect of *Re F* on operations for sterilisation, as well as other matters relating to the sexuality of people with learning disabilities (mental handicap).

15.23 The Law Commission has included a review of aspects of the law relating to mental incapacity in its Fourth Programme of Law Reform (Cm 800). (See *Mentally Incapacitated Adults and Decision-Making: An Overview*, Law Commission Consultation Paper No. 119, HMSO, 1991, and three papers which form the second round of the Law Commission's consultation process: *Mentally Incapacitated Adults and Decision-Making: A New Jurisdiction*, Law Commission Consultation Paper No. 128, *Mentally Incapacitated Adults and Decision Making: Medical Treatment and Research*, Law Commission Consultation Paper No. 129, and *Mentally Incapacitated Adults and Other Vulnerable Adults: Public Law Protection*, Law Commission Consultation Paper No. 130, all HMSO, 1993.)

Treatment of those with capacity to consent where consent is not given

15.24 Ordinarily, a patient capable of giving consent can only be given medical treatment for mental disorder against his wishes in accordance with the provisions of Part IV of the Act. On rare occasions involving emergencies, where it is not possible immediately to apply the provisions of the Mental Health Act, a patient suffering from a mental disorder which is leading to behaviour that is an immediate serious danger to himself or to other people may be given such treatment as represents the minimum necessary response to avert that danger. It must be emphasised that the administration of such treatment is not an alternative to giving treatment under the Mental Health Act nor should its administration delay the proper appliction of the Act nor should its administration delay the proper application of the Act to the patient at the earliest opportunity. (see Chapter 18).

16 Medical treatment and second opinions

(Paras 189–205 of the Memorandum)

General

16.1 The common law (see Chapter 15) applies to patients detained under the Mental Health Act except where specific provision is made in Part IV of the Act. Part IV of the Act provides specific statutory authority for forms of medical treatment for mental disorder to be given to most patients liable to be detained without their consent in certain circumstances and with certain safeguards. It also provides specific safeguards. Patients liable to be detained are those who are detained or have been granted leave of absence (Section 17). It also provides specific safeguards to all patients when treatments are proposed that give rise to special concern.

16.2 The provisions of Part IV can be summarized as follows:

a. *Treatments requiring the patient's consent and a second opinion (section 57)* – psychosurgery and the surgical implantation of hormones for the reduction of male sexual drive (these safeguards apply also to informal patients).

b. *Treatments requiring the patient's consent or a second opinion (section 58)* – the administration of medicine beyond three months and treatment by E C T at any time. These safeguards apply to all patients liable to be detained except those detained under S.4, S.5(2) or (4), S.35, S.135, S.136 and S.37(4); also patients conditionally discharged under S.42(2) and S.73 and 74. All these patients can only be treated under common law.

c. *Treatments that do not require the patient's consent (section 63)* – all medical treatments for mental disorder given by or under the direction of the patient's responsible medical officer and which are not referred to in section 57 or 58 (this provision applies to the same patients as section 58).

d. *Urgent treatment (section 62)* – in certain circumstances the provisions of section 57 and 58 do not apply where urgent treatment is required (see para 16.18 below). The types of treatment and categories of patients to which sections 57 and 58 apply are set out in para 16.2.a & b above and section 62 is not applicable to any other forms of treatment or to any other categories of patient.

16.3 Everyone involved in the operation of Part IV of the Mental Health Act should be familiar with:

a. the provisions of Part IV of the Act;

b. paras 189–205 of the Memorandum;

c. D H S S circular D D L (84)4.

In addition r m os should obtain copies of 'Advice to Second Opinion Appointed Doctors' published by the Mental Health Act Commission.

16.4 Detained status of itself does not imply inability to give consent. For all treatments proposed for a detained patient, and which may be lawfully given under the Act, it is necessary first to seek the patient's agreement and consent. It is the personal responsibility of the patient's r m o to ensure that the patient's valid consent has been sought and the interview at which such consent was sought should be properly recorded.

16.5 Part IV of the Act applies only to medical treatment for mental disorder. Treatments for physical disorder therefore cannot be given under this Part of the Act unless it is a physical disorder that gives rise to a mental disorder and it is necessary to treat the physical disorder in order to treat the mental disorder.

Treatments requiring consent and a second opinion (section 57)

16.6 Section 57 reflects public and professional concern about particular forms of treatment; such treatments need to be considered very carefully in view of the possible long-term effects and the ethical issues that arise. Procedures for implementing this section must be agreed between the Mental Health Act Commission and the hospitals concerned.

16.7 Before the r m o or doctor in charge of treatment refers the case to the Mental Health Act Commission:

a. the referring doctor should personally satisfy himself that the patient is capable of giving valid consent and has consented;

b. the patient and (if the patient agrees) his family and others close to him should be told that the patient's willingness to undergo treatment does not necessarily mean that the decision to proceed has yet been taken. The patient should be made fully aware of the provisions of section 57;

c. for psychosurgery, the consultant considering the patient's case should have fully assessed the patient as suitable for psychosurgery;

d. for psychosurgery, the patient's case should be referred to the Commission prior to his transfer to the neuro-surgical centre for the operation. The Commission organises the attendance of two appointed persons and a doctor. The appointed persons and the doctor will usually visit and interview the patient at the referring hospital at an early stage in the procedure;

e. for surgical implantation of hormones for the purpose of reducing male sexual drive, the relationship of the sexual disorder to mental disorder, the nature of treatment, the likely effects and benefits of treatment and knowledge about possible long-term effects require considerable care and caution should be taken.

16.8 It should be remembered that section 57 only refers to the surgical implantation of hormones for the reduction of male sexual drive where it is administered as a medical treatment for mental disorder; and that, if there is any doubt as to whether it is a mental disorder which is being treated, independent legal and medical advice must be sought. The advice of the Mental Health Act Commission should also be obtained about arrangements for implementing section 57 where necessary.

Treatments requiring consent or a second opinion (section 58)

E C T

16.9 When E C T is proposed valid consent should always be sought by the patient's r m o:

a.　if the patient consents the r m o or the Second Opinion Appointed Doctor (S O A D) should complete form 38 and include on the form the proposed maximum number of applications of E C T. Such information should be included in the patient's treatment plan;

b.　if the patient's valid consent is not forthcoming the r m o (in the event that he wishes to proceed with the treatment) must comply with the requirements of section 58, which should be initiated as soon as possible.

16.10 Whenever practicable, staff should give a patient treated by E C T a leaflet which helps him to understand and remember, both during and after the course of E C T, the advice given about its nature, purpose and likely effects. This may help ensure that a valid consent is in force.

Medication before 3 months

16.11 This period starts on the occasion when medication for mental disorder was first administered by any means during any period of continuing detention (see para 16.13 below). The medication does not necessarily have to be administered continuously throughout the three month period. The patient's r m o must ensure that the patient's valid consent is sought prior to the administration of any medication. If such consent is not forthcoming or is withdrawn during this period, the r m o must consider, if he wishes to proceed in the absence of consent, alternative treatment or give no further treatment.

Medication after 3 months (section 58)

16.12 At the end of the three month period referred to above the patient's r m o should personally seek the patient's consent to continuing medication, and such consent should be sought for any subsequent administration of medication. If the patient consents, the r m o must certify accordingly (form 38). The r m o should indicate on the certificate the drugs proposed by the classes described in the British National Formulary (B N F), the method of their administration and the dose range (indicating the dosages if they are above

B N F advisory maximum limits). If the patient's consent is not forthcoming the r m o must comply with the safeguard requirements of section 58 (although for urgent treatment section 62 may apply).

The 3 months rule

16.13 The 3 month period gives time for the doctor to create a treatment programme suitable for the patient's needs. Although the patient can be treated in the absence of consent during this period no such treatment should be given in the absence of an attempt to obtain valid consent. The three month period is not affected by renewal of the detention, withdrawal of consent, leave or change in or discontinuance of the treatment. A fresh period will only begin if there is a break in the patient's liability for detention.

16.14 If medication is likely to be continued beyond the 3 month period the need for consent or a second opinion should be foreseen in good time. The r m o should satisfy himself at all times that consent remains valid.

Withdrawal of consent

16.15 A patient subject to the provisions of Part IV of the Act may withdraw consent at any time. Fresh consent or the implementing of section 58 procedures is then required before further treatment can be carried out or reinstated. Where the patient withdraws consent he should receive a clear explanation (recorded in the patient's records) of:

- the likely consequences of not receiving the treatment;

- (where applicable) that a second medical opinion under Part IV of the Act may or will be sought in order to authorise treatment in the continuing absence of the patient's consent;

- (where applicable) the doctor's power to begin or continue treatment under section 62 until a second medical opinion has been obtained.

Treatments not requiring the patient's consent (section 63)

16.16 Apart from treatments specifically mentioned in sections 57 and 58, other forms of medical treatment for the mental disorder from which the patient is suffering (so long as they are given by or under the direction of the patient's r m o) may be given without the patient's consent being obtained (although it should always be sought). Section 63 covers a wide range of therapeutic activities involving a variety of professional staff and includes in particular psychological and social therapies (see section 145 for a definition of medical treatment).

16.17 In practice, it is unlikely that most of these activities could be undertaken without the patient's acceptance and active cooperation. Acceptance in relation to such procedures requires a clear expression of agreement between the patient and the therapist before the treatment has begun, such agreement being expressed positively in terms of willingness to co-operate rather than as a consequence of passive submission.

Urgent treatment

16.18 Any decision to treat a patient urgently under section 62 is a responsibility of the patient's r m o who should bear in mind the following considerations:

a. Treatment can only be given where it is immediately necessary to achieve one of the objects set out in section 62 and it is not possible to comply with the safeguards of Part IV of the Act. It is insufficient for the proposed treatment to be simply 'necessary' or 'beneficial.'

b. In certain circumstances 'hazardous' or 'irreversible' treatment cannot be administered under this section even if it is immediately necessary. The patient's r m o is responsible for deciding whether treatment falls into either of these categories, having regard to mainstream medical opinion.

c. Urgent treatment given under section 62 can only continue for as long as it is immediately necessary to achieve the statutory objective(s).

d. Before deciding to give treatment under section 62 the patient's r m o should wherever possible discuss the proposed urgent treatment with others involved with the patient's care.

It is essential that r m os have a clear understanding of the circumstances when section 62 applies (see para 16.2.d).

16.19 The Managers should ensure that a form is devised to be completed by the patient's r m o every time urgent treatment is given under section 62. Such a form should require details to be given of the proposed treatment; why it is of urgent necessity to give the treatment; the length of time for which the treatment was given. The Managers should monitor the use of section 62 in their hospitals.

Review of treatment

16.20 *All* treatments (whether or not section 61 applies to them) should be regularly reviewed and the patient's treatment plan should include details of when this will take place. Where a patient is receiving treatment under section 58(3)(a) (i e the patient has consented and form 38 been completed), the form 38 should always have been completed by either the patients r m o or the S O A D. Although the Act does not direct review of the validity of form 38s, it is good practice for them to be reviewed at regular intervals. When such review is carried out and it is found that the conditions are satisfied, a new form 38 should be completed, if appropriate. If the patient no longer consents and it is considered that the treatment should still be given, a second opinion must be sought.

Review of treatment (section 61)

16.21 When a patient has been treated under section 57 or section 58 (when a Second Opinion Appointed Doctor has authorised treatment in the absence of the patient's consent), a review by the Mental Health Act Commission on behalf of the Secretary of State has to take place:

a. in the circumstances set out in section 61 (all professionals involved should be familiar with the procedures for completing form M H A C 1);

b.   where the S O A D has time limited his certificate or made his certificate conditional upon making of a review report on the treatment at a date earlier than the first statutory review (See M H A C 1).

Once the treatment has been reviewed and form M H A C 1 completed, a copy of that form should be given to the patient.

16.22 When submitting a report under section 61, the r m o should advise the Mental Health Act Commission if a patient for whom a certificate of second opinion has previously been issued has since given his consent and the consent is still valid. After a receipt of a review report, the Mental Health Act Commission will, when required, send an appointed doctor to reassess the patient and decide whether the treatment should continue.

Responsibilities for operating Part IV

16.23 Promoting the welfare of the patient by the implementation of Part IV and its safeguards requires careful planning and management. The patient's r m o is personally responsible for ensuring that Part IV procedures are followed in relation to that patient.

16.24 Overall responsibility for ensuring that the powers and duties of the Act are lawfully obeyed rests with the Managers who should ensure that proper arrangements are made to enable r m os to discharge their responsibilities, but all professional staff involved with the implementation of Part IV of the Act should be familiar with its provisions and the procedures for its implementation in the hospital.

16.25 Patients have a statutory right to be informed about the provisions of Part IV of the Act as it relates to them. They should be reminded by letter in addition to receiving the statutory leaflet when either their consent to treatment is needed or a second opinion is due.

Arranging the visit of the S O A D

16.26 Where it is required, the patient's r m o has the personal responsibility of ensuring that the request for the visit of a S O A D is made. He should ensure that the arrangements are made with the Mental Health Act Commission.

Preparing for the S O A D's visit

16.27 The patient's treatment proposal (together with any records of discussion among relevant professional staff) must be given to the S O A D before or at the time of his visit. The Managers in consultation with the r m o are responsible for ensuring that the patient is available to meet the S O A D and that the following people are available in person (although it is recognised that in exceptional circumstances this may not be possible) at the time the S O A D vists:

- the patient's r m o;

- the statutory 'consultees' (see para 16.34);

- any other relevant persons.

And that the following documents are available:

- the primary copies of the patient's detention documents wherever possible or copies of such documents (in which case the primary document should be available for viewing by the S O A D if he requests);

- all the patient's case notes (records of past responses to similar treatment are very important).

It is desirable that a single professional record is kept for each patient which contains all records relating to that patient. Adequate facilities must be made available for the visit.

The visit of the S O A D

16.28 During his visit the S O A D should:

a. in the case of a treatment under section 58, satisfy himself that the patient's detention papers are in order;

b. interview the patient in private (but others may attend if the patient and the S O A D agree or if it is concluded that the doctor would be at significant risk of physical harm from the patient);

c. discuss the case with the patient's r m o face to face, though in exceptional circumstances telephone consultation will suffice;

d. consult with two other persons professionally concerned with the patient's care as statutorily required (i e the 'statutory consultees'). The S O A D should be prepared, where appropriate, to consult a wider range of persons professionally concerned with the patient's care than those required by the Act and (with the patient's consent) the patient's nearest relative or other appropriate relatives or supporters.

16.29 The S O A D may not be able to reach a decision at the time of the first visit. In these circumstances the patient should be told of the delay.

16.30 Once a decision has been reached, it is the r m o's responsibility to inform the patient of the S O A D's decision.

16.31 Every attempt should be made by the r m o and the S O A D to reach agreement. If the r m o and the S O A D are unable to reach agreement, the patient's r m o should be informed by the S O A D personally at the earliest opportunity. It is good practice for the S O A D to give reasons for his dissent. Neither doctor should allow a disagreement in any way to prejudice the interests of the patient. If agreement cannot be reached, the position should be recorded in the patient's case notes by the r m o who will continue to have responsibility for the patient's management. The opinion given by the S O A D is his personal responsibility. It cannot be appealed against to the Mental Health Act Commission.

16.32 If the patient's situation subsequently changes the r m o may contact the Mental Health Act Commission and request a further second opinion. In these circumstances it is the policy of the Commission to ask the same S O A D to return.

Roles and responsibilities – the hospital Managers

16.33 In anticipation of, and preparation for, a consultation under Part IV, the Managers and their staff should ensure that:

a. the statutory documents are in order and available to the S O A D;

b. a system exists for reminding the r m o prior to the expiry of the limit set by section 58 and section 61 and for checking the doctor's response;

c. a system exists for reminding the patient towards the expiry of the '3 month period' that his consent or a second opinion is required;

d. appropriate personnel are available for consultation. The need for there to be a person other than a doctor or nurse professionally concerned with the patient's care must be foreseen and their involvement initiated well in advance of any consultation.

Roles and responsibilities – the 'statutory consultees'

16.34 The S O A D must consult:

a. a nurse, who must be qualified (nursing assistants, auxiliaries and aides are excluded) and who has been professionally concerned with the patient's care;

b. another person similarly concerned who is neither a nurse nor a doctor. A student nurse, nursing aide, auxiliary or assistant would not be permissible under this latter category but a social worker, occupational therapist, psychologist, psychotherapist etc would be.

16.35 Any person whom the S O A D proposes to consult must decide if he is sufficiently concerned professionally with the patient's care to fulfil the function. If he feels that another person is better placed to fulfil the function, or he is not qualified, he should make this known to the patient's r m o and the S O A D in good time.

16.36 Both consultees may expect a private discussion (only in exceptional cases on the telephone) with the S O A D and to be listened to with consideration.

16.37 Amongst the issues that the 'consultees' should consider commenting upon are:

  – the proposed treatment and the patient's ability to consent to it;

  – other treatment options;

- the way in which the decision to treat was arrived at;

- the facts of the case, progress, attitude of relatives etc;

- the implications of imposing treatment upon a non-consenting subject and the reasons for the patient's refusal of treatment;

- any other matter relating to the patient's care on which the 'consultee' wishes to comment.

'Consultees' should ensure that they make a record of their consultation with the S O A D which is placed in the patient's records.

The role of the S O A D

16.38 The role of the S O A D is to provide an additional safeguard to protect the patient's rights. He must at the time of the interview determine whether the patient is capable of consenting and giving valid consent, or, if the patient does not give his consent or is not capable of giving his consent, whether the treatment proposed by the patient's r m o is likely to alleviate or prevent a deterioriation of the patient's condition and should be given.

16.39 The S O A D acts as an individual and must reach his own judgement as to whether the proposed treatment is reasonable in the light of the general consensus of appropriate treatment for such a condition. In reaching his judgement he should consider not only the therapeutic efficacy of the proposed treatment but also (where a capable patient is withholding his consent) the reasons for such withholding, which should be given their due weight.

16.40 The S O A D should seek professional opinion about the nature of the patient's disorder and problems, the appropriateness of various forms of treatment, including the proposed treatment, and the patient's likely response to different types of treatment especially if based on previous experience of comparable treatment of a similar episode of disorder. He should give due weight to the opinion, knowledge, experience and skill of those consulted. He will have to sign form 39 before treatment may be given without consent. He may direct that a review report on the treatment be sent from the Mental Health Act Commission at a date earlier than the next date for review under section 61.

17 Part III of the Mental Health Act – patients concerned with criminal proceedings

Treatment and care in hospital

Patients on remand to hospital under sections 35 and 36

17.1 A patient who is remanded to hospital for reports or for treatment is entitled to obtain, at his own expense, an independent report on his medical condition from a registered medical practitioner chosen by him for the purpose of applying to court for the termination of the remand. Managers should help in the exercise of this right.

17.2 The consent to treatment provisions of the Act do not apply to patients remanded under section 35, so in the absence of the patient's consent treatment can only be administered in an emergency under the provisions of the common law. (See Chapter 15).

17.3 Where a patient remanded under section 35 is thought to be in need of medical treatment for mental disorder under Part IV of the Act, the patient should be referred back to court as soon as possible with an appropriate recommendation, and with an assessment of whether the patient is in a fit state to attend court. If there is a delay in securing a court date (for example an order under section 36 can only be made by a Crown Court and there can be a considerable delay before the patient is committed to the Crown Court), and depending on the patient's mental condition, consideration should be given to whether the patient meets the criteria for detention under section 3 of the Act.

17.4 A report prepared in pursuit of a section 35 remand order should contain:

– a statement as to whether a patient is suffering from a specified form of mental disorder as required by the section, identifying its relevance to the alleged offence. The report must not anticipate the outcome of proceedings to establish guilt or innocence, and it may be right to suggest that a further report be submitted to the court between (possible) conviction and sentence;

– relevant social factors;

– any recommendations on care and treatment, including where and when it should take place and who should be responsible.

Information

17.5 The Managers have a duty to give information to the patient's nearest relative (unless the patient objects). This should be exercised with care; while in prison the patient will have been invited to give details of parents or next of kin, but this may not be the 'nearest relative' under the Act.

18 Patients presenting particular management problems

18.1 Patients (both detained and informal) or people who may become patients, may behave in such a way as to disturb others around them, or their behaviour may present a risk to themselves or others around them or those charged with their care. These problems may occur anywhere, and the issues addressed here relate to general health care settings as well as psychiatric facilities. It is important to distinguish:

– the needs of patients who pose an immediate threat to themselves or those around them and where techniques for the immediate control of a difficult situation must be used; and

– the need for some patients to remain in a secure environment as a result of a perceived risk to the general public or as a result of pending or past decisions of the courts, but who pose no threat to those around them.

Behaviour contributing to problems in management

18.2 The majority of people do not behave in a disturbing way, and professionals should not assume that a previous history of disturbance means that the patient will always behave that way. Professionals should also recognise that though they may experience the disturbed behaviour as intermittent, fellow residents or carers will experience it through 24 hours. Tolerance to irritating or disturbed behaviour is clearly related to exposure to it, and professionals should not categorise behaviour as disturbed without taking account of the circumstances under which it occurs.

18.3 Behaviour which can give rise to management problems can include:

- refusal to participate in treatment programmes;
- prolonged verbal abuse and threatening behaviour;
- destructive behaviour;
- self-injurious behaviour;
- physical attacks on others.

Possible causes

18.4 In exploring preventive methods staff should be aware of some possible, often very evident causes of problem behaviours:

- boredom and lack of environmental stimulation;
- too much stimulation, noise and general disruption;
- overcrowding;
- antagonism, aggression or provocation on the part of others;
- a generally unsuitable mix of patients;
- the rewarding of undesirable behaviour by attention;
- the inability to protect oneself against harm as a result of mental disorder.

General preventive measures

18.5 In addition to individual care plans much can be done to prevent behaviour problems by examining the ward or other environment and pinpointing problem areas. Among such general measures are:

- keeping patients fully informed of what is happening and why;
- giving each patient a defined personal space and a secure locker for the safe keeping of possessions;
- ensuring access to open space;

– organising the ward (in hospital) to provide quiet rooms, recreation rooms and visitor's rooms;

– ensuring access to a telephone;

– providing structured activities by professional staff;

– encouraging energetic activities for younger patients;

– providing training for staff in the management of disturbed behaviour;

– monitoring the mix of patients;

– developing nurse-patient allocation systems;

– consistent application and monitoring of any individual programme;

– ensuring that patients' complaints are dealt with quickly and fairly.

Restraint

18.6 Restraint may take many forms and may vary in degree from a mild instruction to seclusion. The purpose of restraint is first to take immediate control of a dangerous situation and second to contain or limit the patient's freedom for no longer than is necessary to end or reduce significantly the threat to himself or those around. The most common reasons for restraint are:

– physical assault;

– destructive behaviour;

– non-compliance with treatment;

– self harm or risk of physical injury by accident;

– extreme and prolonged over-activity likely to lead to physical exhaustion.

Basic principles

18.7 The basic principles which should underlie any methods which are aimed at reducing and eliminating unwanted behaviour are:

a.   by intervention, to reduce such behaviour;

b.   to review regularly any intervention as part of the patient's agreed treatment programme relating to his particular management problem.

Where it is likely that, in a group of patients, problem behaviour may appear unpredictably, an agreed strategy for dealing with the unanticipated events should be developed.

Training

18.8 Staff in N H S hospitals and private mental nursing homes who are ordinarily likely to find themselves in situations where control and restraint might be necessary should attend an appropriate course run by a qualified instructor.

Methods of restraining behaviour

18.9 *Physical restraint* should be used as little as possible. Restraint which involves either tying or hooking a patient (whether by means of tape or by using a part of the patient's garments) to some part of a building or to its fixtures or fittings should never be used. Staff must make a balanced judgment between the need to promote an individual's autonomy by allowing him to move around at will and the duty to protect him from likely harm. In every case where the physical freedom of an individual is curtailed in his own interests, staff should record the decision and the reasons for it and state explicitly in a care plan under what circumstances restraint may be used, what form the restraint may take and how it will be reviewed. Every episode of restraint must be fully documented and reviewed.

18.10 Restraining aggressive behaviour by physical means should be done only as a last resort and never as a matter of course. It should be used in an emergency when there seems to be a real possibility that significant harm would occur if intervention is withheld. Any initial attempt to restrain aggressive behaviour should, as far as the situation will allow, be non-physical:

a.   assistance should be sought by call system or verbally;

b. one member of the team should assume control of the incident;

c. the patient should be approached where possible and agreement sought to stop the behaviour, or to comply with a request;

d. where possible an explanation should be given of the consequences of refusing the request from staff to desist;

e. other patients or people not involved in the use of restraint should be asked to leave the area quietly.

18.11 Where non-physical methods have failed or the incident is of such significance as to warrant immediate action, the person in control of the incident may decide to restrain the patient physically. In doing so the following rules should be borne in mind:

a. make a visual check for weapons;

b. nominate staff members to assist in control and allocate each a specific task;

c. a large number of staff grabbing at people can be counter-productive;

d. fewer, but well briefed staff are likely to be more effective;

e. aim at restraining arms and legs from behind if possible, seek to immobilise swiftly and safely;

f. constantly explain reason for action and enlist support from patient for voluntary control as soon as possible;

g. avoid neck holds;

h. avoid excess weight being placed on any area, but particularly stomach and neck;

i. do not slap, kick or punch.

Any restraint must be 'reasonable in the circumstances'. It must be the minimum necessary to deal with the harm that needs to be prevented.

Restraint and complaints

18.12 The Managers should appoint a senior officer, possibly the nominated complaints officer, who should be informed of any patient who is being subjected to any form of restraint that lasts for more than two hours. On receipt of such information, such an officer should as soon as practicable see the patient and then, at regular interviews, make contact with the patient to ascertain if he has any complaints and to assist in putting them forward. In certain circumstances it may be desirable for the officer to devolve this responsibility to another person professionally concerned with the patient's case and with whom the patient has a good working relationship.

Policy on restraint

18.13 Health authorities and N H S trusts should have clear, written policies on the use of restraint.

Medication

18.14 The control of behaviour by medication requires careful consideration. The judicious use of appropriate medication to reduce excitement and activity in order to facilitate other interventions can be an important adjunct to an individual programme. But medication which begins as purely therapeutic may, by prolonged routine administration, become a method of restraint. It is therefore necessary to review each individual case and consider at the outset whether, where medication would have to be administered by force, it would be lawful and therapeutic in the longer term. Medication should not be used as an alternative to adequate staffing levels.

Seclusion

18.15 Seclusion is the supervised confinement of a patient alone in a room which may be locked for the protection of others from significant harm. It is not a procedure that is specifically regulated by statute. Seclusion should be used as little as possible and for the shortest possible time. Many hospitals have discontinued its use. Seclusion should not be used as a punitive measure or to enforce good behaviour. Although it falls within the definition of medical treatment in the Mental Health Act (section 145), seclusion is not a treatment technique and should not feature as part of any treatment programme. Its use therefore cannot be foreseen. It should not be used because of staff shortages or because, for example, equipment is being damaged. Seclusion is a last resort, when all reasonable steps have been taken to avoid its use. It should never be used where there is a risk that the patient may take his own life or otherwise harm himself; its sole aim therefore is to contain severely disturbed behaviour which is likely to cause harm to others.

18.16 Hospitals should have clear written guidelines on the use of seclusion, distinguishing between seclusion and time out (see Chapter 19). The guidelines should contain instructions on environmental standards, the roles and responsibilities of all members of staff, the procedures for recording, monitoring, reviewing and follow-up, including the provision of any care and support to the patient rendered necessary by their seclusion. The aim of the guidelines should be to ensure the safety and well-being of the patient in a dignified and humane environment.

Procedure for seclusion

18.17 The decision to use seclusion can be made in the first instance by a doctor, the nurse in charge of the ward, a nursing officer or senior nursing officer. Where the decision is taken by someone other than a doctor, then the necessary arrangements must be made for a doctor to attend immediately.

18.18 A nurse should be readily available within sight and sound of the seclusion room at all times throughout the period of the patient's seclusion, and present at all times with a patient who has been sedated.

18.19 The aim of observation is to ascertain the state of the patient and whether seclusion can be terminated. The level should be decided on an individual basis, but a documented report must be made every 15 minutes.

18.20 *If seclusion needs to continue* a review should take place very 2 hours, carried out by 2 nurses in the seclusion room, and every 4 hours by a doctor. If seclusion continues for more than 8 hours consecutively or for more than 12 hours intermittently over a period of 48 hours, an independent review must take place with a consultant or other doctor of suitable seniority, a team of nurses and other health care professionals who were not directly involved in the care of the patient at the time the incident which led to the seclusion took plate. If there is no agreement on ensuing action the matter should be referred to the unit general manager.

Conditions of seclusion

18.21 Seclusion should be in a safe, secure and properly identified room, where the patient cannot harm himself, accidentally or intentionally. The room should have adequate heating, lighting, ventilation and seating. It is a matter for local judgement what the patient is allowed to take into the room, but he should always be clothed.

18.22 The room should offer complete observation from the outside, while also affording the patient privacy from other patients.

Record keeping

18.23 Detailed records should be kept in the patient's case notes of any use of seclusion, the reasons for its use and subsequent activity, cross-referenced to a special seclusion book or forms which should contain a step-by-step account of the seclusion procedure in every instance. The principal entry should be made by the nurse in charge of the ward and the record should be countersigned by a doctor and a unit nursing manager. The Managers should monitor and regularly review the use of seclusion.

Locking ward doors on open wards

18.24 The management, security and safety of patients should, wherever practicable, be ensured by means of adequate staffing. Authorities are responsible for trying to ensure that staffing is adequate to prevent the need for the practice of locking patients in wards, individual rooms or any other area.

18.25 The nurse in charge of any shift is responsible for the care and protection of patients and staff, and the maintenance of a safe environment. This responsibility includes the care of patients who have been detained in hospital because they are considered a danger to other people. At his discretion, the nurse in charge may decide for all or part of the shift for which he is responsible to lock the door of the ward because of the behaviour of a patient or patients to keep the environment safe. When doing that he should:

a. inform all staff of why he is taking this action and how long it will last;

b. inform the patient or patients whose behaviour has led to the ward door being locked of the reason for taking such action;

c. inform all other patients that they may leave on request at any time and ensure that someone is available to unlock the door;

d. inform his line manager of his action;

e. inform the r m o or nominated deputy;

f. keep a record of this action and reasons, and make use of an incident reporting procedure.

18.26 When handing over to the relieving shift the nurse in charge should discuss in detail the reasons for his action. Where the relieving nurse considers it necessary to keep the door locked, (a) to (e) above apply. Where any ward is locked for three consecutive shifts (excluding night duty) the unit general manager should be informed.

18.27 The safety of informal patients, who would be at risk of harm if they were allowed to wander out of a ward or nursing home at will, can usually be secured by means of adequate staff and good surveillance. Combination locks and double handled doors to prevent mentally frail elderly people or people with learning disabilities (mental handicap) from wandering out should be used as little as possible and only in units where there is a regular and significant risk of patients wandering off accidentally and, as a result, being at risk of harm. There should be clear unit policies on the use of locks and other devices and a mechanism for reviewing decisions. Every patient should have an individual care plan which states explicitly why and when he will be prevented from leaving the ward. Patients who are not deliberately trying to leave the ward, but who may wander out accidentally may legitimately be deterred from leaving the ward by those devices. In the case of patients who persistently and purposely attempt to leave a ward or nursing home, whether or not they understand the risk involved, consideration must be given to assessing whether they would more appropriately be formally detained under the Act in the hospital or a registered mental nursing home rather than remain as informal patients.

Locked wards and secure areas

18.28 There are some detained patients in ordinary psychiatric hospitals who may be liable to cause danger to themselves or others. For these patients, professional judgement or the requirement of a Court as an alternative to imprisonment, may point to the need for varying degrees of security. In such cases, where the need for physical security is a prerequisite, the patient's r m o, in consultation with the multi-disciplinary team should ensure that:

a. he has carefully weighed the patient's individual circumstances and the degree of danger involved;

b. he has carefully assessed the relative clinical considerations of placing the patient in a physically secure environment; in addition to or as opposed to providing care by way of intensive staffing;

c. treatment in secure conditions lasts for the minimum necessary period;

d. the patient's bed on an open ward is retained at all times to minimise any delay to his returning there.

18.29 It would be desirable for authorities/N H S trusts to ensure that:

a. a ward/area is specifically designated for this purpose with appropriate staffing levels;

b. written guidelines are provided, setting out and clearly distinguishing between the categories of patient where it is appropriate to use physically secure conditions and those where it is not. The guidelines should include a clear policy for the practice, proper procedures and safeguards, the justification for its use and the circumstances in which it can be used.

Observation and care of patients at risk of self injury

18.30 Patients may reasonably expect that they will be protected from harming themselves when the drive to self injury is a result of mental disorder for which they are receiving care and treatment. All patients should be assessed on admission for their expressed wish to harm themselves and/or suicidal tendencies and evidence sought of past or recent behaviour which suggests they may currently be at risk. Individual care plans should include a clear statement of the degree of risk of self-harm, what level of observation is warranted to protect the patient and at what interval the level of observation will be reviewed. Staff must balance the potentially distressing effect on the patient of close observation, particularly when one-to-one observation is proposed for many hours, against the risk of self injury. Levels of observation and risk should be regularly reviewed and a record made of agreed decisions.

Deprivation of day-time clothing

18.31 Patients should never be deprived of appropriate day-time clothing during the day, with the intention of restricting their freedom of movement. They should not be deprived of other aids necessary for their daily living.

Staff

18.32 Staff must try and get to know patients not only in order for the patient to gain confidence in them but also so that they can learn to recognise potential danger signs in patients and be able to diffuse the situation in time. They should have good communication skills and know when to intervene in certain potentially aggressive situations. Continuity of staffing is an important factor both in the development of professional skills and consistency in managing patients.

Managers

18.33 Staff involved in control and restraint may experience a degree of stress. Managers should ensure that they are given the opportunity to discuss these issues with them (the Managers) and with colleagues. Managers should formulate and make available to health authority, N H S trust and local authority staff and to local authority management a clear written operational policy on all forms of restraint.

19 Psychological treatments

Psychological treatments

19.1 A wide variety of psychological treatment techniques are used in the treatment of people suffering from mental disorder, including a variety of types of psychotherapy on an individual and group basis and behaviour modification techniques which have their origin in the application of learning theory and research. Behaviour modification techniques often form a part of the care and treatment of people with learning disabilities (mental handicap) and other people who through cognitive impairment have difficulty in learning new behaviours through normal intellectual understanding. Some treatments can interfere with patients' basic rights. This is most obviously so in the case of some behaviour modification programmes as dealt with below. However, other forms of psychological treatment can do the same. For example, group therapy has the potential to release powerful group pressures which may coerce individuals to act in ways that they find upsetting or distressing, such as discussing sensitive and embarrassing material in a context they would avoid if it were possible to do so. This can lead to a reasonable concern for confidentiality. Similarly individual psychotherapy can be coercive and distressing if poorly conducted. Behaviour modification programmes have possibly most potential for harm if poorly designed. No treatment should deprive a patient of food, shelter, water, warmth, a comfortable environment, confidentiality or reasonable privacy (both physical and in relation to their personal feelings and thoughts). Psychological treatments should be conducted under the supervision of those properly trained in the use of the specific methods employed.

Behaviour modification programmes

19.2 The Managers must ensure that the behaviour modification programmes are set out clearly, methodically and in such a way that they can be understood by staff, patients and relatives. Guidelines should include procedures for noting and monitoring their use. Managers should keep themselves well informed of up to date research in this area. A person with sufficient skills in implementing behaviour modification programmes should be available to monitor procedures as well as the progress of patients.

19.3 Any programme to be used should form part of a patient's previously agreed treatment plan. At no time should it be used as a spontaneous reaction to a particular type of behaviour. The patient's consent should always be sought (see para 19.7).

19.4 A decision to use any behaviour modification programme for an individual patient should be preceded by a full discussion with the professional staff concerned with the patient.

19.5 Such a programme should be regularly reviewed in the case of each patient, and abandoned if it has proved ineffective or otherwise modified if necessary.

19.6 Patients and their relatives should be fully informed of the planned use of any such methods as part of a patient's treatment and the patient's consent should always be sought.

19.7 Although such treatments may proceed in the absence of a patient's consent, this should only be done in certain carefully justified circumstances. If consent is not or cannot be given a locally agreed procedure should be adopted in which the r m o should seek the advice of a suitably qualified person who is not a member of the clinical team responsible for the patient. This will normally be a psychologist although some medical staff, social workers or nurses may have received special training that equips them to supervise psychological procedures. The r m o in these circumstances should notify the management of the hospital, unit or registered mental nursing home of the details of the plan of treatment. (See also Chapter 15)

19.8 The r m o can delegate appropriate members of staff to use such programmes. It is therefore the r m o's responsibility to ensure that those to whom he has delegated this have adequate skills and abilities to carry out the procedures to the required standard. The professional managers must ensure that such members of staff have received relevant training and that they know who to turn to for advice where necessary.

Time out

19.9 Time out is a behaviour modification technique which denies a patient for a period (lasting from a few seconds to no more than 15 minutes) opportunities to participate in an activity or to obtain positive reinforcers following (normally immediately) an incident of unacceptable or unwanted behaviour, and which then returns the patient to his original environment. Time out should never include the use of a locked room. Time out should be clearly distinguished from seclusion, which is for use in an emergency only and should never form part of a behavioural programme. All staff working in units which use behaviour modification techniques must be familar with the principles of time out and the distinction between time out and seclusion. Time out should not normally take place in a room which is used for seclusion on other occasions. It should be seen as one of a range of planned methods of managing a difficult or disturbed patient, and not as a spontaneous reaction to such behaviour.

19.10 Hospitals should have clear written policies on the use of time out as part of their overall policy on general management. The guidelines should include a clear definition of this form of therapy and procedures for noting and monitoring its use on individual patients.

19.11 The important principles of time out are:

a.   to enable the patient, if his behaviour is changed, to lead a less restricted life within his usual surroundings or any other setting to which he is likely to go;

b.   to form part of a programme where the achievement of positive goals is as much part of the treatment plan as reducing unwanted behaviour.

20   Leave of absence (section 17)

(Paras 72–73 of the Memorandum)

20.1 Leave of absence can only be authorized in accordance with the provisions of section 17. It can be an important part of a patient's treatment plan. It is important to note that only the patient's r m o (with the approval of the Home Secretary in the case of restricted patients) can grant a detained patient leave of absence. The granting of leave should not be used as an alternative to discharging the patient.

20.2 The patient should be fully involved in the decision to grant leave and must be asked to consent to any consultation with others (e g relatives, professionals in the community) thought necessary before leave is granted. He should be able to demonstrate to his professional carers that he is likely to cope outside the hospital.

20.3 Leave of absence should be well planned (if possible well in advance) and involve detailed consultation with any appropriate relatives/friends (especially where the patient is to reside with them) and commuity services which could contribute to its successful implementation. If relatives/friends are to be involved in the patient's care, but he does not consent to their being consulted, leave should not be granted. It should be remembered that the duty to provide aftercare (section 117 – see Chapter 27) applies to patients on leave of absence.

20.4 **The power to grant leave (section 17)**

a. Unrestricted patients
(1) The decision (which cannot be delegated to another professional) rests with the patient's r m o after necessary consultation (it is not a decision that can be devolved to another doctor), who may impose such conditions as he considers necessary. The r m o and other professionals involved should bear in mind, however, that their responsibilities for the patient's care remain the same while he is on leave although they are exercised in a different way. Similarly the aftercare provisions of section 117 apply to a patient on leave of absence;

(ii) it is a common practice for the r m o, after multi-disciplinary discussions, to authorise short-term local escorted leave at the discretion of nursing staff. Whilst flexibility to respond to day to day changes in a patient's condition is helpful in rehabilitation, there is no formal authority for the r m o to delegate his power under section 17. He must, therefore, accept responsibility for any leave arranged with his general approval;

(iii) where the r m o authorizes nurses to arrange discretionary local leave this fact must be recorded. Hospitals should consider the use of a simple record form on which the r m o can authorise leave and specify the conditions attached to it. See para 20.5.

b. Restricted patients

Any proposal to grant leave has to be approved by the Home Secretary who should be given as much notice as possible, together with full details of the proposed leave.

Recording and information

20.5 The granting of leave and the conditions attached to it should be recorded in the patient's notes and copies given to the patient, any appropriate relatives/friends and any professionals in the community who need to know.

Revoking leave of absence

20.6 An unrestricted patient's leave can be revoked by his r m o where he considers it is necessary, in the interests of the patient's health or safety or for the protection of other people, that the patient should again become an in-patient. The r m o must consider very seriously the reasons for recalling a patient and the consequences or effects that a revocation of leave may have on him. A refusal to take medication should not on its own, for example, be a reason for revocation. The r m o must arrange for a notice in writing revoking the leave to be served on the patient or on the person for the time being in charge of the patient. The reasons for recall should be fully explained to the patient and a record of such explanation placed in the patient's case notes. A restricted patient's leave may be revoked either by his r m o or the Home Secretary.

20.7 It is essential that any appropriate relatives/friends (especially where the patient is residing with them whilst on leave) and other professionals in the community who need to know should have easy access to the patient's r m o if they feel it is essential for consideration to be given to the return of the patient to hospital before the patient's leave is due to end.

Medical treatment while on leave

20.8 A patient granted leave under section 17 remains 'liable to be detained' and the provisions of Part IV of the Act continue to apply unless he is a patient referred to in section 56(1). If it becomes necessary to administer treatment in the absence of the patient's consent under Part IV, the patient should be recalled to hospital.

Duration of leave/renewal of authority to detain

20.9 A period of leave cannot last longer than the duration of the authority to detain which was current when leave was granted. If the patient has not been recalled from leave at the end of the period of detention, he ceases to be liable to be detained. If the r m o decides to recall the patient before the end of the period of detention, he should be satisfied that the patient needs medical treatment in hospital.

20.10 It is unlawful to recall from leave a patient subject to section 3 solely in order to renew the authority to detain the patient. (R v Hallstrom, Ex Parte W and R v Gardiner, Ex Parte L (1986) 2 WLR 883).

21 Absence without leave (section 18)

(Paras 76–80 and 288–289 of the Memorandum)

21.1 The hospital must know the address of a person on leave of absence.

21.2 It is the responsibility of the Managers and of the local authority where guardianship is concerned to ensure that there is a clear written policy in relation to action to be taken when a detained patient or a patient subject to guardianship goes absent without leave.

21.3 All staff should be familiar with the policy as well as paras 76–80 and 288–289 of the Memorandum.

21.4 In particular the policy should include guidance as to:

a. the immediate action to be taken by any members of staff who become aware that a patient has gone absent without leave, including the requirement that they immediately inform the nurse in charge of the patient's ward who should in turn ensure that the patient's r m o is immediately informed;

b. the circumstances when a search of the hospital and its grounds should be initiated;

c. in the case of a patient detained in hospital, circumstances when the police should be informed (having regard to para 288 of the Memorandum);

d. how and when the patient's nearest relative should be informed. In almost all cases the patient's nearest relative should be informed immediately the patient goes absent without leave and any exceptions to this requirement should be clearly set out in the policy;

e. in the case of someone received into guardianship who is absent without leave from the place where he is required to reside, the person in the local social services authority to be notified immediately.

22 Managers' duty to review detention (section 23)

22.1 Managers' review is the process by which the Managers decide whether a patient can still be detained or can be discharged. Chapter 24 below deals with the definition of the Managers in the Act. The Managers' review is a different procedure from referral to a Mental Health Review Tribunal and the Managers are responsible for ensuring that patients understand the difference. **It is important** that no impression is given to patients that any application to a Mental Health Review Tribunal must be preceded by a Managers' review nor that a request for a Managers' review negates the patient's rights to apply to a Mental Health Review Tribunal.

22.2 **Managers should undertake a review**, at any time at their discretion, but must do so:

a. when the patient requests it, unless there has recently been a review and there is no evidence that the patient's condition or other relevant factors have changed. In these latter circumstances the Managers should investigate, and if there is any doubt a review should take place;

b. when the patient's r m o makes a report to the Managers, in accordance with section 20. It is recommended that such reports should be received not less than two weeks prior to the expiry of relevant periods of detention, to enable the patient's detention to be reviewed as close as possible to the expiry date of detention;

c. where a patient's r m o makes a report to the Managers in accordance with section 25(1), barring a nearest relative's discharge application.

Responsibilities before the review

22.3 The Managers should ensure that they have reports from the patient's r m o and other relevant disciplines, (such as social workers, psychologists, occupational therapists and nursing staff involved in the patient's care), and they should consult with those professionals concerned with the patient's care, where they think it necessary after reading these reports.

22.4 If the patient consents, Managers must ensure that the patient's nearest and/or most concerned relatives are informed of the review and asked to comment or to be available for interview in the same way as when the patient is to appear before a Mental Health Review Tribunal. If the patient withholds consent the Managers should ask the appropriate professional concerned with the patient's care to obtain the views of the patient's nearest relative and/or most concerned relatives, and include these in their reports to the Managers.

The review

22.5 It is for the Managers to decide how to review bearing in mind that the following are necessary.

a. to balance informality and the gravity of the task; they are reviewing a patient's continued detention;

b. to help the patient to explain why he wishes to be discharged;

c. to allow the patient to be accompanied by a member of staff, friend or representative of his choosing, to help put his point of view;

d. to ensure that the patient's r m o and other relevant pro-fessionals are actively and positively questioned by the Managers;

e. to ensure (subject to para 22.4 above) that the patient's nearest/ most concerned relatives are given the opportunity to give their point of view or to have it represented through an A S W, C P N or any other such person. The patient must always be offered the opportunity of speaking to the Managers alone;

f.   if the patient so wishes, to enable the patient and other parties to the review to hear each other's accounts to the Managers and to put questions to each other.

After the review

22.6 The Managers should ensure that their decision and the reasons for it are communicated immediately, both orally and in writing, to the patient, to any relative who has expressed views, and to the relevant professionals. At least one of the Managers reviewing the patient's detention should explain to the patient in person the reason for their decision, and copies of the report prepared for the review together with the Managers' written decision letter should be placed in the patient's records.

23 Complaints

General

23.1 The Hospital Complaints Procedure Act 1985 places a duty upon health authorities to investigate any complaint on the part of a patient about any aspect of his treatment. The Department of Health and Welsh Office circulars HC(88)37 and WHC(88)36 respectively, issued in June 1988, set out both the duties and procedures for making complaints and for their investigation.

The Managers' duties

23.2 The Managers should ensure that as part of their training, all staff are fully conversant not only with the requirements and procedures of the Hospital Complaints Procedure Act, but also with the patient's rights to make complaints to the Mental Health Act Commission. In accordance with HC(88)37/WHC(88)36, the Managers must ensure the nomination of a complaints officer within their establishment. One of the duties of this officer should be to log complaints and to ensure that patients are notified of the outcome.

Staff

23.3 Staff have the responsibility of bringing to the attention of all patients, both orally and in writing, the procedures for making a complaint through the hospital complaints system, and, in relation to detained patients, their rights to complain to the Mental Health Act Commission. If a patient is unable to formulate his complaint, he should be given reasonable assistance to do so by staff. It is the personal responsibility of all members of staff involved in a patient's care to give such assistance where necessary.

Recording

23.4 All patients' case notes should contain accounts of any complaints made and the outcome in every instance.

24 Duties of the hospital Managers

(Paras 62–63 of the Memorandum)

24.1 The Managers have important statutory powers, responsibilities and duties concerning detained patients, and are specifically defined in the 1983 Mental Health Act (section 145).

24.2 The Managers, as defined in the Act are:

a. in relation to a hospital vested in the Secretary of State and in relation to any accommodation provided by a local authority and used as a hospital by or on behalf of the Secretary of State under the Act, the district health authority or special health authority responsible for the administration of the hospital;

b. in relation to a special hospital, the special health authority established to carry out the functions of the Secretary of State;

c. in relation to a mental nursing home registered in pursuance of the Registered Homes Act 1984, the person or persons registered in respect of the home;

d. in relation to a hospital vested in a National Health Service trust, the directors of the trust.

24.3 Officers are those persons properly authorized by the Managers to act on their behalf.

24.4 The health authority should appoint a committee or sub-committee to undertake the duties of the Managers. The committee or sub-committee should comprise informed members of the health authority and/or other appointed and informed outside persons. In an N H S trust those duties have to be carried out by the directors of the trust (see footnote)[1]. Any person who acts as a Manager should be fully informed about the functions of Managers.

---

[1] In relation to N H S trusts, at the time of publication, legal advice is that the current definition of managers requires the function of discharging patients to be performed by three or more non-executive directors (one of whom may be the Chairman) in person. The Department has written to trusts to explain this more fully (T E L 93/2). It will be seeking the earliest possible amendment to the Act to permit delegation to a committee.

24.5 In respect of mental nursing homes the function of discharging patients may be exercised in accordance with the following:

a. in the case of patients who are not N H S patients, the Managers of the mental nursing home may delegate the function to a committee or sub-committee;

b. in the case of patients maintained under contract with a health authority, the power of discharge may be exercised on their behalf by a committee or sub-committee of the authority which may include informed outside persons.

24.6 The Managers may delegate to officers many of their statutory tasks under Part II of the Act, but excluding the function of discharging patients. It is the duty of Managers to ensure that all officers acting on their behalf are competent to undertake their delegated duties. The Managers retain the ultimate responsibility for the execution of all such duties.

Admission

24.7 It is the Managers' duty to ensure that the grounds for admitting the patient are valid and reasonable and that all relevant admission documents are in order. The authorized or delegated officer should be able to make judgements based on the facts available regarding the need for admission. Where a patient is admitted under the Act following an application by their nearest relative, the Managers should request the relevant Local Authority Social Services Department to provide them with a social circumstances report (section 14).

Transfer

24.8 Subject to the provisions of section 19 of the Act and the Mental Health (Hospital, Guardianship and Consent to Treatment) Regulations 1983 (SI 1983 No 893), the Managers can exercise the power to transfer under the Act certain categories of detained patients to another hospital administered by the same authority, to a special health authority or to a hospital in another district. The delegated officers must be able fully to justify their reasons for so doing and ensure that such a transfer is not for punitive reasons.

Scrutiny and receipt of documents

24.9 The Managers should ensure that those formally delegated to receive documents and all those who will be required to scrutinize admission documents have a thorough knowledge of the Act. (See Chapter 12)

24.10 Documents received and scrutinized should, as a matter of good practice, include the order in writing by a r m o to discharge a patient from detention.

Rectification of documents

24.11 Section 15 of the Act allows for the rectification of certain errors contained in admission documents with the consent of the Managers. It is for the nominated officer to consider whether the papers can be rectified and where possible to take the necessary steps. (See Chapter 12)

Detention, review, discharge

24.12 The Managers have the power to discharge certain categories of detained patients. They should ensure that reviews of the patient's detention take place not just at the time stipulated in section 20 of the Act, but whenever it is thought necessary and in particular, shortly after a patient's admission. (See Chapter 22)

24.13 Section 23 provides that the r m o may discharge a detained patient by giving an order in writing. Managers should ensure that a suitable form is available upon which this order can be given and that it is received and acknowledged by someone authorised to receive documents on behalf of the Managers (see paras 24.6 and 24.9).

The giving of information

24.14 The Managers have statutory obligations concerning the giving of information to both detained patients (section 132) and their nearest relatives (section 133) (see Chapter 14).

Correspondence of patients

24.15 The Managers of the special hospitals have statutory powers (section 134) to withhold outgoing and incoming mail in certain circumstances. The Managers should have a written policy concerning the implementation of these powers; this should be discussed with the Mental Health Act Commission which has the power to review any decision to withhold mail (section 121(7)). The outgoing mail of *any* detained patient may be withheld if the person to whom it is addressed makes such a request in writing to the Managers, the patient's r m o or the Secretary of State.

Access to Mental Health Review Tribunals

24.16 The Managers should ensure that any patient who wishes to apply to a Mental Health Review Tribunal is given all necessary assistance to progress such an application. Under section 68 of the Mental Health Act, they are obliged to refer certain patients detained under Part II of the Act to Mental Health Review Tribunals and it is the responsibility of the Managers to ensure that the necessary arrangements are made. Such referrals should be made within one week after renewal of the patient's detention. (see paras 209 and 210 of the Memorandum).

25   Personal searches

25.1 Authorities should ensure that there is an operational policy on the searching of patients and their belongings. Such a policy should be checked with the health authority's legal advisers.

25.2 It should not be part of such a policy routinely to carry out searches of patients and their personal belongings. If, however, there are lawful grounds for carrying out such a search, the patient's consent should be sought. In undertaking such a search staff should have due regard for the dignity of the person concerned and the need to carry out the search in such a way as to ensure the maximum privacy.

25.3 If the patient does not consent to the search, staff should consult with the unit general manager (or such other delegated senior staff (e g senior nurse manager) when he is not available) before undertaking any lawful search. The same principles relating to the patient's dignity and the need for maximum privacy apply. Any such search should be carried out with the minimum force necessary and in the case of a search of a patient's person, unless urgent necessity dictates otherwise, such a search should be carried out by a staff member of the same sex.

25.4 If items belonging to a patient are removed, the patient should be informed where these are being kept.

26 Visiting patients detained in hospital or registered mental nursing homes

The right to be visited

26.1 All detained patients are entitled to maintain contact with and be visited by whomsoever they wish, subject only to some carefully limited exceptions. The prohibition of a visit by a person whom the patient has requested to visit or agreed to see should be regarded as a serious interference with the rights of the patient and to be taken only in exceptional circumstances (see below). A decision to exclude a visitor should only be taken after other means to deal with the problem have been fully explored. Any decision to exclude a visitor should be fully documented and available for independent scrutiny by the Mental Health Act Commission.

Grounds for excluding a visitor

26.2 There are two principal grounds which may justify the exclusion of a visitor:—

a. Restriction on clinical grounds

It will sometimes be the case that a patient's relationship with a relative, friend or supporter is anti-therapeutic (in the short or long term) to an extent that discernible arrest of progress or even deterioration in the patient's mental state is evident and can reasonably be anticipated if contact were not to be restricted. Very occasionally, concern may centre primarily on the potential safety of a particular visitor to a disturbed patient. The grounds for any decision by the r m o (which should only be taken after full discussion with the patient's multi-disciplinary care team) should be clearly documented and explained to the patient and the person concerned.

b. Restriction on security grounds

The behaviour or propensities of a particular visitor may be, or have been in the past, disruptive or subversive to a degree that exclusion from the hospital or mental nursing home is necessary as a last resort. Examples of such behaviour or propensities are: incitement to abscond, smuggling of illicit drugs/alcohol into the hospital, mental nursing home or unit, transfer of potential weapons, or unacceptable aggression or unauthorised media access. A decision to exclude a visitor on the grounds of his behaviour or propensities should be fully documented and explained to the patient and, where possible and appropriate, the person concerned.

Facilitation of visiting

26.3 Inflexibility on the part of the hospital or mental nursing home should not be allowed to be an unnecessary deterrent to regular visiting as deemed to be desirable or reasonable by the patient, his visitors and those responsible for his treatment, albeit within the legitimate time constraints of his therapeutic programme. Ordinarily, inadequate staff numbers should not be a deterrent to regular visiting. Failure to provide appropriate and congenial facilities should not be a deterrent to regular visiting. Particular consideration needs to be given to the problems associated with the distance visitors may have to travel, which is often encountered with regional and supra-regional facilities.

Other forms of communication

26.4 Every effort must be made to assist the patient, where appropriate, to make contact with relatives, friends and supporters. In particular patients should have readily accessible and appropriate daytime telephone facilities and no restrictions should be placed upon dispatch and receipt of their mail over and above those referred to in section 134 of the Act.

Managers

26.5 Managers should regularly monitor the exclusion from the hospital or mental nursing home of visitors to detained patients.

27   Aftercare

27.1 The purpose of aftercare is to enable a patient to return to his home or accommodation other than a hospital or nursing home, and to minimize the chances of him needing any future in-patient hospital care.

27.2 Section 117 of the Act requires health authorities and local authorities, in conjunction with voluntary agencies, to provide aftercare for certain categories of detained patients.

27.3 Health authorities, N H S trusts and social services authorities should, together with local voluntary organisations, agree procedures for establishing proper aftercare arrangements. In the case of patients detained under section 37/41 or section 47/49 there will be special considerations to be taken into account.

27.4 Proper records should be kept of all those patients for whom section 117 could apply and of those for whom arrangements have been made under section 117. These records could be in the form of a register.

27.5 Managers in the health service, N H S trusts and Directors of Social Services should ensure that all staff are aware of the care programme approach as laid down in Circular HC(90)23/ LASSL(90)11 and the principles set out in the Welsh Office Mental Illness Strategy.

27.6 When a decision has been taken to discharge or grant leave to a patient, it is the responsibility of the r m o to ensure that a discussion takes place to establish a care plan to organise the management of the patient's continuing health and social care needs. This discussion will usually take place in multi-professional clinical meetings held in psychiatric hospitals and units. If this is not possible, administrative support should be available to the r m o to assist in making arrangements.

Who should be involved

27.7 Those who should be involved in the discussion are:

— the patient's r m o;

— a nurse involved in caring for the patient in hospital;

— a social worker specialising in mental health work;

— the G P;

— a community psychiatric nurse;

— a representative of relevant voluntary organisations (where appropriate and available);

— the patient if he wishes and/or a relative or other nominated representative.

27.8 Professionals should be made available to attend. Representatives of housing authorities should be invited if accommodation is an issue. It is important that those who are involved are able to take decisions regarding their own and as far as possible their agencies' involvement. If approval for plans needs to be obtained from more senior levels (for example, for funding), it is important that this causes no delay to the implementation of the plans.

Consideration for aftercare

27.9 Those contributing to the discussion should consider the following issues:

a.   the patient's own wishes and needs;

b.   the views of any relevant relative, friend or supporter of the patient;

c.   the need for agreement with an appropriate representative at the receiving health authority if it is to be different from that of the discharging authority;

d. the possible involvement of other agencies, e g probation, voluntary organisations;

e. the establishing of a care plan, based on proper assessment and clearly identified needs, in which the following issues must be considered and planned insofar as resources permit: day care arrangements, appropriate accommodation, out-patient treatment, counselling, personal support, assistance in welfare rights, assistance in managing finances, and, if necessary, in claiming benefits;

f. the appointment of a key worker from either of the statutory agencies to monitor the care plan's implementation, liaise and co-ordinate where necessary and report to the senior officer in their agency any problems that arise which cannot be resolved through normal discussion;

g. the identification of any unmet need.

27.10 The multi-professional discussion should establish an agreed outline of the patient's needs and assets taking into account his social and cultural background, and agree a time-scale for the implementation of the various aspects of the plan. All key people with specific responsibilities with regard to the patient should be properly identified. Once plans are agreed it is essential that any changes are discussed with others involved with the patient before being implemented. The plan should be recorded in writing.

27.11 The care plan should be regularly reviewed. It will be the responsibility of the key worker to arrange reviews of the plan until it is agreed that it is no longer necessary. The senior officer in the key worker's agency responsible for section 117 arrangements should ensure that all aspects of the procedure are followed.

28 Part III of the Mental Health Act – patients concerned with criminal proceedings

Leaving hospital

Discharge/return to court

28.1 Conditionally discharged restricted patients – supervision

Those involved in the supervision of a conditionally discharged restricted patient should have copies of and be familiar with 'Supervision and After-Care of Conditionally Discharged Restricted Patients' (HO/DoH notes of guidance (1987)) and Recall of mentally disordered patients subject to Home Office restrictions on discharge (HSG(93)20/LAC(93)9).

Recall

28.2 If a conditionally discharged restricted patient requires hospital admission, it will not always be necessary for the Home Secretary to recall the patient to hospital. For example:

a. The patient may be willing to accept treatment informally. In these circumstances, however, care should be taken to ensure that the possibility of the patient being recalled does not render the patient's consent to informal admission invalid by reason of duress.

b. In some cases it may be appropriate to consider admitting the patient under Part II of the Act as an alternative.

c. It may not always be necessary to recall the patient to the same hospital from which he was conditionally discharged. In some cases recall to a hospital with a lesser (or greater) degree of security will be appropriate.

28.3 When a recall is being considered this should be discussed between the doctor and the social supervisor.

28.4 If a patient is recalled, the person taking him into custody should explain that he is being recalled to hospital by the Home Secretary and that a fuller explanation will be given to him later. As soon as possible after admission to hospital, and in any event within 72 hours of admission, the r m o or his deputy and A S W or a representative of the hospital management should explain to the patient the reason for his recall and ensure, in so far as the patient's mental state allows, that he understands. The patient should also be informed that his case will be referred to a Mental Health Review Tribunal within one month.

28.5 The patient's r m o should ensure that:

— the patient is given assistance to inform his legal adviser (if any);

— subject to the patient's consent, his nearest relative and/or other appropriate relative or friend is told.

28.6 Patients on remand/subject to interim hospital orders

All professionals concerned with ensuring the return to court of a patient on remand or under an interim hospital order should be familiar with the contents of paras 31–33 of Home Office circular number 71/1984. When a patient has been admitted on remand or subject to an interim hospital order, it is the responsibility of the hospital to return the patient to court as required. The court should give adequate notice of the hearing. The hospital should liaise with the courts in plenty of time to affirm the arrangements for escorting the patient to/from hospital. The hospital will be responsible for providing a suitable escort for the patient when he is taken from the hospital to the court and should plan for the provision of necessary staff to do this. The assistance of the police may be requested if necessary. Once on the court premises, the patient will come under the supervision of the police or prison officers there.

29 People with learning disabilities (mental handicap)

General

29.1 The guidance given elsewhere in the Code applies to patients with learning disabilities (or mental handicap). This chapter gives guidance on a number of particular issues of importance to this group of patients.

29.2 Very few people with learning disabilities are detained under the Act. Some admission sections can only be considered where the person with a learning disability falls within the legal definition of 'mental impairment' or 'severe mental impairment'. People with learning disabilities can be considered for admission under the Act when they are suffering from another form of mental disorder (for example mental illness).

Communication

29.3 The assessment of a person with learning disabilities requires special consideration to be given to communication with a person being assessed. Where possible the A S W should have had experience of working with people with learning disabilities or be able to call upon someone who has. It is important that someone who knows the patient, and can communicate with him, is present at the assessment. Someone with a knowledge of Makaton or other communication system may be of assistance.

Assessment

29.4 It is desirable that no patient should be classified under the Act as mentally impaired or severely mentally impaired without an assessment by a consultant psychiatrist in learning disabilities and without a formal psychological assessment. This assessment should be part of a complete appraisal by medical, nursing, social work and psychology professionals and, wherever appropriate, by those with experience in learning disabilities in consultation with a relevant relative, friend or supporter of the patient. This procedure is also desirable where it is proposed that a patient is to be detained under section 2 on the grounds of mental disorder in the form of arrested or incomplete development of mind, although the urgency of the case may preclude this.

Mental impairment/severe mental impairment (legally defined in section 1)

29.5 The identification of an individual who falls within these legal categories is a matter for clinical judgement, guided by current professional practice and subject to the relevant legal requirements. Those assessing the patient must be satisfied that the person concerned displays a number of characteristics difficult to define in practice. This section of the chapter sets out guidance in relation to the key factors or components of these legal categories.

Incomplete or arrested development of mind. This implies that the features that determine the learning disability were present at some stage which permanently prevented the usual maturation of intellectual and social development. It excludes persons whose learning disability derives from accident, injury or illness occurring after that point usually accepted as complete development.

Severe or significant impairment of intelligence. The judgement as to the presence of this particular characteristic must be made on the basis of reliable and careful assessment.

Severe or significant impairment of social functioning. The evidence of the degree and nature of social competence should be based on reliable and recent observations, preferably from a number of sources such as social workers, nurses and psychologists. Such evidence should include the results of one or more social functioning assessment tests.

Abnormally aggressive behaviour. Any assessment of this category should be based on observations of behaviour which lead to a conclusion that the actions are outside the usual range of aggressive behaviour, and which cause actual damage and/or real distress occurring recently or persistently or with excessive severity.

Irresponsible conduct. The assessment of this characteristic should be based on an observation of behaviour which shows a lack of responsibility, a disregard of the consequences of action taken, and where the results cause actual damage or real distress, either recently or persistently or with excessive severity.

30 Children and young people under the age of 18

General

30.1 The Code of Practice applies to all patients including those under 18. This chapter gives guidance on a number of issues of particular importance to those under the age of 18. There is no minimum age limit for admission to hospital under the Act.

30.2 Practice for this age group should be guided by the following principles:

a. young people should be kept as fully informed as possible about their care and treatment; their views and wishes must always be taken into account;

b. unless statute specifically overrides, young people should generally be regarded as having the right to make their own decisions (and in particular treatment decisions) when they have sufficient 'understanding and intelligence';

c. any intervention in the life of a young person considered necessary by reason of their mental disorder should be the least restrictive possible and result in the least possible segregation from family, friends, community and school;

d. all children and young people in hospital should receive appropriate education.

30.3 The legal framework governing the admission to hospital and treatment of young people under the age of 18 (and in particular those under the age of 16) is complex and it is the responsibility of all professionals and the relevant local health authorities and N H S trusts to ensure that there is sufficient guidance available to those responsible for the care of children and young people.

30.4 Whenever the care and treatment of somebody under the age of 16 is being considered, the following questions (amongst many others) need to be asked:

a. which persons or bodies have parental responsibility for the child (to make decisions for the child)? It is essential that those responsible for the child or young person's care always request copies of any court orders (wardship, care order, residence order (stating with whom the child should live), evidence of appointment as a guardian, contact order, etc.) for reference on the hospital ward in relation to examination, assessment or treatment.

b. if the child is living with either of the parents who are separated, whether there is a residence order and if so in whose favour;

c. what is the capacity of the child to make his own decisions in terms of emotional maturity, intellectual capacity and psychological state? (see Chapter 15);

d. where a parent refuses consent to treatment, how sound are the reasons and on what grounds are they made?;

e. could the needs of the young person be met in a social services or educational placement? To what extent have these authorities exhausted all possible alternative placements?;

f. how viable would be treatment of an under 16 year old living at home if there was no parental consent and no statutory orders?

Informal admission to hospital by parents or guardians

30.5 *Children under 16.* Parents or guardians may arrange for the admission of children under the age of 16 to hospitals as informal patients. Where a doctor concludes, however, that a child under the age of 16 has the capacity to make such a decision for himself, there is no right to admit him to hospital informally or to keep him there on an informal basis against his will.[1]

---

[1] But see *Re R (A Minor) (Wardship Consent to Treatment)* [1991] 3 W L R 592.

Where a child is willing to be so admitted, but the parents/guardian object, their views should be accorded serious consideration and given due weight. It should be remembered that recourse to law to stop such an admission could be sought.

30.6 *Young people aged 16–17.* Anyone in this age group who is 'capable of expressing his own wishes' can admit or discharge himself as an informal patient to or from hospital, irrespective of the wishes of his parents or guardian.[2]

Consent to medical treatment

30.7 The following guidance applies to young people who are not detained under the Act:

a. *Under 16.* If a child has 'sufficient understanding and intelligence' he can take decisions about his own medical treatment in the same way as an adult.[3] Otherwise the permission of parents/ guardians must be sought (save in emergencies where only the treatment necessary to end the emergency should be given). If parents/guardians do not consent to treatment, consideration should be given to both the use of the child care legislation and the Mental Health Act before coming to a final conclusion as to what action should be taken. Under section 100 of the Children Act 1989 a local authority may also seek leave to ask the High Court to exercise its inherent jurisdiction to make orders with respect to children, if the conditions set out in section 100(4) are met.

b. The same principles concerning consent apply where the under 16 year old is in the care of a local authority. Where such a child does not have sufficient 'understanding and intelligence' to take his own treatment decisions, treatment can be authorised by any person or body with parental responsibility. A local authority has parental responsibility for a child in its care, i e under a care order. Wherever possible, parents should be consulted. However local authorities can in the exercise of their powers under section 33(3)(b) of the Children Act 1989 limit the extent to which parents exercise their parental responsibility. In certain pre-Children Act

---

[2] But see *Re W* (A Minor) (Medical Treatment: Court's Jurisdiction) [1992] 3 W L R 758.
[3] But see Re R and Re W above.

wardships, although the children are deemed to be in care within the meaning of section 31 of the Children Act 1989, court directions may still require treatment decisions to be agreed by the court. Where children are wards of court (and also not deemed to be subject to a care order under section 31 of the Children Act 1989) the consent of the High Court must be sought. In an emergency consent may be obtained retrospectively (but this should be regarded as wholly exceptional).

c. *Young people aged 16 and 17.* Young people in this age group who have the capacity to make their own treatment decisions can do so in the same way as adults (section 8 Family Law Reform Act 1969). Where such a young person does not have this capacity the authorisation of either parent, guardian or care authority (whichever has the lawful authority in relation to the particular young person) must be obtained. The consent of the High Court must be obtained in the case of wards of court.

d. *Refusal of a minor to consent to treatment.* No minor of whatever age has power by refusing consent to treatment to override a consent to treatment by anyone who has parental responsibility for the minor including a local authority with the benefit of a care order or consent by the court. Nevertheless such a refusal is a very important consideration in making clinical judgements and for parents and the court in deciding whether themselves to give consent. The importance increases with the age and maturity of the minor. (See Re W (A Minor) (Medical Treatment: Court's Jurisdiction) [1992] 3 W L R 758 at page 772 – also known as Re J).

e. In cases involving emergency protection orders, child assessment orders, interim care orders and full supervision orders under the Children Act 1989, a competent child has a statutory right to refuse to consent to examination, assessment and in certain circumstances treatment. Such refusal is not capable of being overridden.

Parent/guardians consent

30.8 The fact that a child or young person has been informally admitted by parents/guardians should not lead professionals to assume that they have consented to any treatment regarded as 'necessary'. Consent should be sought for each aspect of the child's care and treatment as it arises. 'Blanket' consent forms must not be used.

Children placed in secure accommodation

30.9 Where a child is looked after by a local authority and placed in accommodation where liberty is restricted (for example N H S secure units or a registered mental nursing home) application must be made to the family proceedings court within 72 hours if the restriction is to last beyond that period (section 25 of the Children Act 1989 and the Children (Secure Accommodation) Regulations 1991 (S I 1991/1505) and the Children (Secure Accommodation) (No 2) Regulations 1991 (S I 1991/2034). Applications are to be made by local authorities if children are looked after by them and by health authorities, N H S trusts, local education authorities or persons running residential care, nursing or mental nursing homes in other cases involving such establishments. These provisions do not apply to such children who are detained under the Mental Health Act 1983. Where the child is a ward of court, the permission of the High Court must be obtained prior to any restriction of liberty. In cases where the Mental Health Act does not apply the criteria to be applied by the wardship court are those contained in section 25 of the 1989 Act and the accompanying Regulations.

Information

30.10 The advice concerning the giving of information (see Chapter 14) applies with equal force to patients under the age of 18. In particular where such patients are detained under the Act, it is important that assistance is given to enable their legal representation at any Mental Health Review Tribunal.

Confidentiality

30.11 Young people's legal rights to confidentiality should be strictly observed. It is important that all professionals have a clear understanding of their obligations and confidentiality to young people and that any limits to such an obligation are made clear to a young person who has the capacity to understand them.

Placement

30.12 It is always preferable for children and young people admitted to hospital to be accommodated with others of their own age group in children's wards or adolescent units, separate from adults. If, exceptionally, this is not practicable, discrete accommodation in an adult ward, with facilities and staffing appropriate to the needs of children and young people, offers the most satisfactory solution.

Complaints

30.13 Children and young people in hospital (both as informal and detained patients) and their parents or guardians should have ready access to existing complaints procedures, which should be drawn to their attention on their admission to hospital. The Managers should appoint an officer whose responsibility it is to ensure that this is done and to assist any complainant. Where a child is being looked after by a local authority, accommodation on behalf of a voluntary organisation or otherwise accommodated in a registered children's home, he will be entitled to use the Children Act complaints procedure established in accordance with the Representations Procedure (Children) Regulations 1991 (S I 1991/894).

Welfare of certain hospital patients

30.14 Local authorities should ensure that they arrange for visits to be made to certain patients (including children and young persons looked after by them whether or not under a care order and those accommodated or intended to be accommodated for three months or more by health authorities, N H S trusts, local education authorities or in residential care, nursing or mental nursing homes – see Review of Children's Cases Regulations 1991 (S I 1991/895) and sections 85 and 86 of the Children Act 1989) quite apart from their duty in respect to children in their care in hospitals or nursing homes in England and Wales as required by section 116. Local authorities should take such other steps in relation to the patient while in hospital or nursing home as would be expected to be taken by his parents. Local authorities are under a duty to promote contact between children who are in need and their families if they live away from home and to help them get back together (paragraphs 10 and 15

119

of Schedule 2 to the Children Act 1989) and to arrange for persons (independent visitors) to visit and befriend children looked after by the authority wherever they are if they have not been regularly visited by their parents (paragraph 17 of Schedule 2 to the Act).

GLOSSARY

The sections referred to are those of the 1983 Mental Health Act.

Act, the	Mental Health Act 1983
Applicant, the	The Patient's nearest relative or an Approved Social Worker (S 11)
Approved Social Worker (A S W)	Defined in S 145(1) (but see S 114)
Community Psychiatric Nurse (CPN)	First reference 2.16
Forms	Details of the forms referred to in the Code of Practice can be found in schedule 1 of Mental Health (Hospital, Guardianship and Consent to Treatment) Regulations 1983 (S I 1983 No 893)
Hospital	Defined in S 145(1)
Local Social Services Authority	Defined in S 145(1)
Managers, the	Defined in S 145(1)
Memorandum, the	Mental Health Act 1983 Memorandum on Parts I to VI, VIII and X. Department of Health (HMSO 1987)
Medical Treatment	See S 145(1)
Mental Disorder (and statutory sub categories of mental disorder)	Defined in S 1
Mental Nursing Home	Defined in S 145(1)

Nearest Relative	Defined in S 26
Nominated Medical Attendant	Defined in S 34(1)
Patient	Defined in S 145(1)
Place of Safety	Defined in S 135(6)
Regulations	A number of regulations (also known as statutory instruments) have been made under powers given in the Act. The most important, for the purposes of understanding this Code are the Mental Health (Hospital, Guardianship and Consent to Treatment) Regulations 1983 (S I 1983 No 893)
Responsible Medical Officer (R M O)	Defined in S 34
Second Opinion Appointed Doctor (S O A D)	See chapter 16

STATUTORY REFERENCES

Children Act 1989

Section

25	30.9
31	30.7
33	30.7
85	30.14
86	30.14
100	30.7

Mental Health Act 1983

Section

1	2.18, 29.5,
2	2.8, 2.9, 2.13, 3.12, 5.1–5.4, 6.8, 29.4
3	2.6, 2.8, 2.9, 3.12, 5.1–5.4
4	6.1–6.8, 16.2
5(2)	8.1–8.12, 16.2
5(3)	8.13–8.16
5(4)	9.1–9.10, 16.2
7	13.1–13.10
11	2.13
12	2.36–2.38, 4.1
13(4)	2.26, 2.27, 2.30, 2.33
14	24.7
15	12.1–12.5, 24.11
17	16.1, 20.1–20.10
18	21.1–21.4
20	22.2, 24.12
23	22.1–22.6, 24.13
25(1)	22.2c
26	2.13
29	2.14
35–55 (Part III)	3.1–3.14
	7.1–7.3
	16.2
	13.10
	17.1–17.5
56–64(Part IV)	16.1–16.40

Section

Police and Criminal Evidence Act 1984

Section

INDEX

Admission:

Aftercare:

Approved Doctors:

Approved Social Workers:

Ethnicity: 2.40

Guardianship:

- assessment for 13.2–13.3
- components for 13.4–13.5
- duties of S S D 13.6
- guardianship under section 37 13.10
- guardianship under section 39A 3.5
- hospitalisation 13.8–13.9
- powers of guardian 13.7
- purpose of 13.1

Health Authorities:

- Hospital Complaints Procedure Act 23.1
- responsibilities for approving doctors 2.36–2.37
- responsibilities for establishing aftercare arrangements 27.3
- responsibilities in relation to the doctors' holding power 8.1

Hormone Implantation:

- need to consult M H A C 16.8

Information:

- children and young people 30.10
- display of information 14.2
- general 14.1–14.2
- Managers' duties 14.6–14.9
- particular information 14.13
- patients with sensory impairment 14.10–14.11
- recording 14.12
- statutory information 14.3–14.5
- who should give information 14.9

Printed in the United Kingdom for HMSO
Dd297561 10/93 C50 G531 10170